WORKING
CAPITAL

How to put your money to work and live entrepreneurially

Gabriel Nardi-Huffman, CFA

AMPHIBIAN

Editing services by Nardi Editorial LLC

Published by Amphibian Books, Brooklyn, NY

ISBN 979-8-218-17878-9

No portion of this book may be reproduced in any form without written permission from the publisher or author, except as permitted by U.S. copyright law. The information provided in this book is for informational purposes only and is not intended to be a source of advice or analysis with respect to the material presented. The information and/or documents contained in this book do not constitute legal or financial advice. The author does not make any guarantee or other promise as to any results that may be obtained from using the content of this book. To the maximum extent permitted by law, the publisher and the author disclaim any and all liability in the event any information, commentary, analysis, opinions, advice, and/or recommendations contained in this book prove to be inaccurate, incomplete or unreliable, or result in any investment or other losses. The author is providing this book and its contents on an "as is" basis. Your use of the information in this book is at your own risk.

For my family, who both inspired me to write this and helped make sure it didn't stink.

CONTENTS

PREFACE

This book evolved out of a ten-page whitepaper I wrote called *Gabe's Quick Guide to Personal Capital*. It encompassed three phases of wealth creation—a knowledge phase, a saving phase and an investment phase—and was the result of having friends and relatives approach me with questions about their finances. I had some questions of my own. Most of what we discussed revolved loosely around a system of managing money. Understanding how savings were being accumulated and what to do with them was at the heart of these conversations. On my own, I had been applying many of these same concepts and building up a framework that seemed to touch on the key areas of wealth creation. By the fifth or sixth conversation, I figured I'd better write it all down.

The *Guide* received solid feedback, which led me to delve deeper into these ideas and expand on the three phases in Part 1, as well as the important topics in Part 2 (debt, housing and taxes). I hope you enjoy reading this book as much as I've enjoyed writing it!

Gabriel Nardi-Huffman, CFA

Brooklyn, New York 2023

PART 1
THE FRAMEWORK

GETTING STARTED

To invest successfully over a lifetime does not require a stratospheric IQ, unusual business insights, or inside information. What's needed is a sound intellectual framework for making decisions and the ability to keep emotions from corroding that framework.

Warren Buffett, *The Intelligent Investor*

Managing personal finances can be stressful. Jargon, math, feeling like savings are slipping away. Economic pundits on television yelling about the Federal Reserve. Wild gyrations in the stock market. But it doesn't have to be this way. Despite the fact that most K-12 schools don't teach personal finance, and many adults lack a professional advisor, the basic concepts of personal money management can be approached, digested, and methodically implemented to produce radically better financial outcomes for anyone with the will to get started.

This book aims to help readers build a rock-solid foundation on which to manage their capital so that their money goes to work for them—rather than the other way around. When our dollars put on their work pants, go out into the world, and make some money for us, we get to reap the benefits of their efforts. Quite a fruitful relationship! It is our job to help those dollars maximize their productivity. Improving our saving and investing techniques and building up a workforce of capital can lead to long-term wealth creation, a higher standard of living, and reduced stress.

At its core, *Working Capital* is a book about improving financial outcomes by building a saving and investing system and thinking entrepreneurially about how to optimize that system. These concepts are the same at any asset or income level—one doesn't have to be rich or enjoy a high income to begin with to implement them. After all, CEOs of large and small companies alike are tasked with creating value out of the same basic set of strategies: understand the business thoroughly, optimize cash flow, and invest surplus cash in attractive areas. These three functions are the key ingredients for creating value.

In the *Working Capital* approach, everyone is the CEO of their personal finances and is tasked with creating higher net worth. Taking a snapshot of our financial position, finding innovative ways to grow revenue and save on cost, and plugging the resulting savings into a strong investment program is how our personal finance enterprise wins over time. And the more we can employ our assets in highly paid "jobs," the more we can spend time doing whatever it is that makes us happy and fulfilled.

A key motivation I had for writing this book was to show that rolling up the sleeves about our money is worth it. Plenty of guides out there talk up sensationalist ideals of wealth creation concepts but are scarce on actual practical advice and underlying theory. This isn't one of those books— we're going to get our hands dirty.

From my own experience, personal finance resources tend to fall into one of three broad categories: (i) saving and budgeting techniques, (ii) investment strategy by and for professionals, and (iii) "feel-good" motivational texts.

The saving and budgeting resources can provide helpful background knowledge and tips for maximizing one's savings rate; however, they often focus primarily on the cost side of things, building and maintaining an airtight budget. Cutting, cutting, and more cutting, rather than maximizing revenue opportunities. The *Working Capital* approach is a bit different. My view is that by focusing on hard work, creativity, and education, the revenue side can be much more fruitful. Being prudent about cost is critical to a strong savings plan. But revenue opportunities are where the real juice is. Cutting costs won't make you rich.

In addition, much of the saving and budgeting literature minimizes time spent on investing, often just suggesting a broad allocation to the market and periodic rebalancing. This advice is helpful, of course, but I don't think it goes far enough, and all too often these resources present a broad market allocation as a substitute or shortcut for having to make active capital allocation decisions. The line of thinking goes that most individuals will not have the desire or time to actively manage their investments, so they should just park their money in an index fund and forget about it. Sometimes the veiled assertion is that investing is a job best left to the pros. I think this misses the point. Regardless of whether the investor takes a more passive or active approach to the actual positions they hold, the truth is that they need to own that capital allocation decision process. They should understand the cost and benefits involved in whatever path they choose and how they expect to profit from their investments. This book aims to arm the individual with the right tools and techniques to chart their own investment path.

By contrast, many of the pure investing books out there were written by professional investors with an at least quasi-professional audience in mind. The jargon can be challenging, and these books often assume that the reader is starting out with a sizable chunk of cash to invest. There is a trove of valuable literature on investing strategy written by the best in the business, but without a solid foundation and a process for generating savings, these texts are by and large inaccessible to most of the population.

While exploring many of the same concepts, my approach starts with a simpler framework, allocating each surplus dollar of cash into a waterfall of investment buckets that grows alongside savings. We will take things step by step, to build an investment portfolio from the ground up and make sure that the foundation is solid enough to maximize the potential for attractive risk-adjusted returns over time (explaining what the heck that phrase means along the way).

The other main category of personal finance literature—the motivational texts—tend to consist of perhaps marginally comforting literary productions that are often composed with the goal of selling books or seminars rather than providing real, practical knowledge to the reader. Unfortunately, we appear to be living in a golden era for hype, and it has never been easier for enterprising gurus to hock their "guaranteed" 25% annualized returns. The best defense against these characters is a sound understanding of investment fundamentals. By understanding the logic and framework behind intelligently saving and investing, the reader should benefit by seeing their stress levels fall in direct proportion to the increase in control over their finances. Wealth creation can enhance our standard of living when approached with a sound foundation. No motivational speeches needed.

In Part 1 of this book, I outline a theory of wealth creation through saving and investing that I have been applying to my own life and that seems to work well over time. That framework is focused around the Three Phases of Wealth Creation:

-   <u>Know the Numbers</u>: we take a look at the basic definitions and concepts underlying most personal finance decisions and outline a strategy for getting organized. Along the way, we pick up some useful accounting skills that help in analyzing our finances.

- Supercharge Savings: we break down the key drivers of savings, namely, revenue and expenses. The goal is to maximize what we get to keep, either by earning more or spending less. Savings are raw material for the investment process. You can't make an omelet without eggs.

- Invest the Surplus: after organizing the financial profile and optimizing the surplus cash saved each month, we figure out ways to make our money work for us. The basic concept is that when our money works harder, we get to work "less hard." We analyze the Three Heroes of Capital Allocation and discuss how to incubate positive long-term investment results while minimizing anxiety—a worthy pursuit!

Afterward, in Part 2, we dig deeper into three cornerstone personal finance topics that play a crucial role in wealth creation: debt, housing, and taxes.

What's the Game, and Why Does It Matter?—Framing Today's Personal Finance Landscape

"You're telling me I learned what the inside of a starfish looks like but not how to put together a budget?"

Far from becoming simpler, easier to navigate, and more accessible, the personal finance landscape has become more complex and challenging for many of us over the last few decades. Important financial "barriers to entry" are working against the working man or woman. These obstacles merit some discussion, because they help frame our objectives as personal capital allocators.

According to CNBC, only 21 states require high school students to take a course that integrates personal finance concepts.[1] Developing sound money management skills is not considered core to most educational curriculums. More than 80% of adults surveyed in a recent study by Chase Bank wished they had learned more about finance growing up.[2]

With minimal formal focus on personal finance in school, it is entirely possible to grow up and live one's life without having learned the basics of saving and investing. That's a problem. The concepts discussed in this book are not groundbreaking, or rocket science, or groundbreaking rocket science. But there is a minimum hump to get over that can mean the difference between confidently saving and investing vs. accumulating anxiety and feeling a lack of control.

Other factors have combined to strain the personal finance landscape.

First is the above-average cost inflation (relative to wage growth) that has taken place in higher education and healthcare.

Over the past 20 years, the availability of federal and private student loan debt has made college attainable for the majority of the population. This is good. Yet, at the same time, higher education costs have grown tremendously, meaning that the financial impact of the decision to go to college is much higher than it once was, necessitating greater borrowing on the part of the student or their parents. This is bad. For example, the Bureau of Labor Statistics estimates that for the 10-year period between 2006 and 2016, higher education costs increased by 63%, or roughly 5% annually on average compared to an overall 21% rise, or 1.9% per year, in consumer prices generally.[3]

---

[1] CNBC: "How Each State Is Shaping the Personal Finance IQ of Its Students."
[2] Survey conducted by OnePoll on behalf of Chase.
[3] Bureau of Labor Statistics: "College Tuition and Fees Increase 63 percent Since January 2006."

While the ease of taking on federal or private sector student loan debt has meant that college is still "attainable" for many people, attainability and affordability are two different things. Many college graduates today are starting out in the red, with average student debt upon graduation of more than $37,000.[4] This puts a pressing burden on young adults to optimize their financial profile rather quickly, as the wealth-destructive impacts of high debt levels can compound over time, just as easily as wealth-building investment returns can.

Hence, we have a seeming paradox in regard to the financial impact of higher education. On the one hand, some students may find they need access to higher education to enhance their long-term earnings power and help jump-start a career. Education in general sits at the core of the wealth creation endeavor in this book—it is absolutely critical. However, the pursuit of that very education can saddle a person with an extremely high debt burden, when they are just starting to work full-time. These dueling forces are arguably at a peak when someone graduates from college or another form of higher education, because their earnings power is at its lowest relative to their financial liability (in the form of student loans, bills, auto loans, etc). A basic understanding of personal finance during that time can go a long way toward setting someone on the right path.

While higher education costs primarily impact younger graduates, healthcare cost inflation has disproportionately impacted the older age cohort. According to data from the Centers for Medicare and Medicaid Services, healthcare spending has increased from roughly 7% of U.S. GDP in 1970 to almost 18% today, meaning that healthcare expenditures are eating up a significantly larger share of household wallets.[5] Most of these costs are necessary rather than discretionary expenditures, because they

---

[4] Debt.org: "Students and Debt."
[5] Peterson-KFF Health System Tracker: "How Has U.S. Spending on Healthcare Changed over Time?"

9

have to do with maintaining one's health, meaning that consumers have little choice but to pay for the care they need. Understanding the root drivers of wealth creation and setting aside money to fund these expenses will help keep healthcare expenditures manageable.

The next reason why an introductory knowledge of personal finance and sound money management is critically important today is the set of perverse incentives in the current financial landscape. Financial advisors and consultants can be very valuable resources and provide key advice around major life events and financial goals. However, many of these advisors are only interested in working with clients who have already built up a sizable amount of capital, because this is what determines how much revenue that advisor can generate from the relationship. This isn't inherently nefarious, but it does mean that the best advice will go to those who already have capital to invest, while those who are just starting out or struggling to pay off debt will have to rely more on their personal networks and ad hoc knowledge-seeking.

According to a joint study by CNBC and Acorns, 75% of those surveyed did not have a professional financial advisor to turn to for help.[6] Ironically, those who lack the adequate savings levels to be attractive to a financial advisor are by definition among those who could benefit the most from professional advice. Leveling the playing field here is what this book is all about.

Further, some investments, such as those in venture capital funds, hedge funds, private equity, and private debt are off-limits to investors who don't meet minimum net worth requirements (known as "accredited investor" standards). Hence, small investors and those just starting out are at a double disadvantage: reduced access to professional advisors and a

---

[6] CNBC: "75 percent of Americans Are Winging It When It Comes to Their Financial Future."

reduced opportunity set of investments. A basic understanding of capital allocation principles is important to help balance the scales.

On a more pleasant note, smaller investors have some completely kick-ass advantages of their own, compared to larger investors and institutions. These advantages are discussed in more detail in later chapters (particularly in Phase 3), however the big ones have to do with the concepts of liquidity and freedom. Small investors have a wide set of investment choices because they don't have to worry about being able to buy and sell in size. Often, institutions are precluded from buying stakes in smaller or less liquid companies where the investment would be hard to sell. Additionally, the small investor doesn't have to worry about someone looking over their shoulder and judging their performance on a quarterly (or even monthly) basis. Instead, he or she can focus on slicing and dicing through the available opportunities to find portfolio constituents with a maximum probability of success.

Further, in today's personal finance environment, vast amounts of information are within a keyboard's reach. Digital brokerages with no minimum asset requirement make the actual investing process cheaper and faster, while broadening the individual's ability to access new markets and asset classes. In short, the process of getting invested and the opportunities to do so have never been better. However, this power can be overwhelming without first having foundational personal finance knowledge and a framework in place to take advantage of it.

The third contributing factor to the strains on today's personal finance landscape is the replacement over time of defined benefit pension schemes with investor-controlled, defined-contribution plans. Historically, company "lifers" could count on collecting a guaranteed pension after retirement. While this is still in practice for some companies today (and factors significantly into the retirement plans for public sector employees who work for federal, state, or local governments), the majority of firms have shifted to defined contribution plans, in which employers contribute to and help administer retirement accounts (such as 401(k) plans) for their employees. In these cases, the employees choose their specific investments themselves.

According to a BLS study released in 2012, the percentage of all workers covered by a pension plan fell by half between 1990 and 2011, from roughly 40% to less than 20%.[7] This has shifted a lot of the risk of investment performance from companies to their employees. Choosing the right investments and contribution amounts requires the kind of personal finance background this book aims to provide.

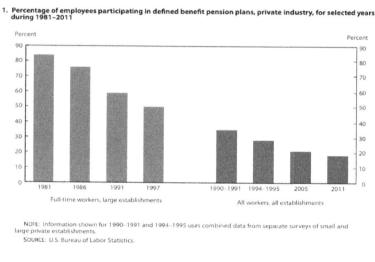

1. Percentage of employees participating in defined benefit pension plans, private industry, for selected years during 1981–2011

NOTE: Information shown for 1990–1991 and 1994–1995 uses combined data from separate surveys of small and large private establishments.
SOURCE: U.S. Bureau of Labor Statistics.

Figure 1.1: Percentage of employees covered by a pension plan.

Finally, although economic crises have existed throughout history, over the past 20 years, savers and investors have had to deal with significantly volatile events: the dot-com boom/bust and the subsequent recession in the early 2000s; the Great Financial Crisis and housing collapse in 2007–2008; and more recently, the Covid-19 pandemic, which

---

[7] Bureau of Labor Statistics: "The Last Private Industry Pension Plans: A Visual Essay."

has upended life around the world in previously unimaginable ways. As globalization increases the international correlation of economies, labor markets and investment returns, the potential for dramatic swings in everyday life and in markets may only increase. With more of the savings and investment risk now borne by the individual, this means that it is more important than ever to have a firm grasp on one's finances in order to successfully ride out the ups and downs.

Having an army reserve of savings intelligently distributed across investments with a high probability of success will always be an important competitive advantage for the individual. Even if we lose a job, the fact that we have our capital going to work for us would keep some income rolling in and give us time to bridge the crisis.

Financial Independence Is Not a Binary Outcome

The textbook definition of financial independence is being able to retire from work and live fully off of one's investment portfolio. I call this immunizing one's cost structure, because all of a person's expenses are accounted for by investment profits. If someone spends $25,000 per year, and that person thinks they can earn 5% on their investments, then they would need $500,000 of assets to immunize their cost structure and not have to work ($500,000 assets * 5% return = $25,000). Their expenses would be entirely matched by their investment profits. Theoretically, if the entire investment portfolio was risk-free government bonds, there wouldn't even be any risk associated with this strategy, although in practice this is rare. More likely, investment returns can only be estimated, and cost structures tend to change over time (a single person in their 20s is going to have a vastly different cost structure than a married couple in their 40s with multiple children and three adopted alien fish), making true financial independence a bit trickier to pin down.

This concept of immunizing our cost structure as representing financial independence may seem a little strange at first. Really what it means is that the more we can cover our liabilities with the returns we earn on investments, then the more we can replace our income from working with investment profits, freeing up time to pursue whatever makes us happiest and most fulfilled, because we know that the bills have been taken care of. That is a powerful result and something worth putting in the time to achieve.

While full cost immunization—as in retirement—is something that many people aspire to, this holy grail of financial independence isn't the only outcome, and I think too many resources emphasize an all-or-nothing approach to financial freedom. What's more, viewing financial independence as a binary outcome and overemphasizing its importance can lead to contorted approaches to saving that optimize for cost cutting instead of wealth creation. Living in a shoebox and never traveling or going out to dinner with friends might lead to financial independence in 15 years rather than 25, but that approach sacrifices a heck of a lot of fun in the meantime. Isn't there a healthier way to approach personal wealth creation?

More aligned with the goal of *Working Capital* is to view financial independence as a spectrum, where the set of financial conditions one has is something that can be improved upon to produce lasting benefits and a more fulfilled life. Everyone sits on a dynamic range of financial independence and moving up or down this range happens over time, meaning that our endeavor is more of a lifelong, gradual improvement process rather than a dichotomy of "haves" and "have-nots." Most of the time, it isn't binary, so it is better to aim yourself at the process rather than the endpoint, and to think about milestones that are relevant to your life (such as being comfortable ordering guacamole with your burrito even though it costs extra). In this way, building a real estate portfolio that produces some cash flow per year could allow someone to cut back on the hours they work and pursue other interests even though they haven't fully immunized their costs. Progress is still progress.

Constructing a system based on the Three Phases of Wealth Creation and becoming the entrepreneurial CEO of one's own personal finances is at the heart of our journey. Aligned with the framework of this book, in Phase 1 we should get a sense of where we sit within the range of financial independence. By Phase 2, we should start moving steadily toward the higher end of the range. Phase 3 provides the rocket fuel that allows us to accelerate up the range, without actually having to pay for the rocket fuel. Boom times.

The First Master Formula

As covered in the chapters ahead, improving financial outcomes by growing personal wealth is really just a function of combining a straightforward saving plan with an appropriate long-term investment strategy. This book provides some foundational knowledge about how to approach each of these and delves into specific strategies that help optimize results within that framework.

It is my hope that by the end of *Working Capital*, readers will be able to develop a simple plan for getting their finances in order and will have done enough groundwork to be able to confidently seek out answers to future finance questions.

In pursuit of that goal, I present several Master Formulas throughout this book. These Master Formulas are more akin to mental models that I think help distill the concepts we discuss rather than mathematically prescriptive phrases that need to be memorized. They simplify our goals into a short form, which readers might find helpful. Here's our first Master Formula.

Master Formula #1:

Wealth Creation = Saving + Investing

All that this first Master Formula says is that the two principal components of wealth creation are saving and investing. Simple. By the end of Phase 2, we should have a pretty good idea of how to maximize savings, which sets the stage well for Phase 3, in which we find ways to invest that surplus. According to Master Formula #1, the resulting wealth creation would be due to the growth in our capital as we earn returns on that "army reserve" of savings by investing intelligently. Note that this comes without having to work any harder in our day-to-day lives. That's why savvy investors are seen as being able to passively increase their standard of living over long periods of time.

The Benefits of Compounding, and Why Starting Early Is a Winning Strategy (and Why Starting Late Is Still a Winning Strategy)

My wealth has come from a combination of living in America, some lucky genes, and compound interest.

Warren Buffett

When it comes to long-term wealth creation, the mechanism of compound interest underpins almost everything we discuss. It is the actual process by which our savings transform into future value, so it is crucial to try and understand.

A familiar allegory describing compound interest goes like this. There once lived a queen who was highly confident in her chess-playing abilities.

She was undefeated (by her count). One day, she challenged a traveling sage to a game and agreed to give him whatever he wanted if he won—a low-probability event, in her mind. If the sage lost, he would bring tidings of her majesty's genius across the land. As fate would have it, the sage won the game with some clever rook play. Capitalizing on his favor, he asked the queen for a single grain of rice, and then for double that amount each day going forward. Day two he received two grains, and day three he was given four grains. Easy enough; rice is small. However, by the thirtieth day—not even a month later—the Queen was paying out over one billion grains of rice per day and had to declare bankruptcy (Goldman Sachs handled the restructuring). This helps illustrate the power of compound interest and the long-term amounts it can deliver from seemingly miniscule starting points.

Let's take an introductory look at this process in action. Without getting too much into the weeds on the formula below (we will be grabbing our Weedwacker in Phase 3), the process of compound interest broadly describes how a starting amount of capital (or "principal") can grow into a larger amount of capital ("future value") over some specific amount of time and for a given rate of return (with that return typically presented on an annualized percentage basis). For our purposes, compounding shows how investment returns can turn a small chunk of change into a very large chunk of change.

A basic formula for compound interest is:

Future Value = Principal * (1+annualized rate of return)^time in years

Breaking down the formula a bit shows the process of how we grow wealth through investing. On the right-hand side, we start with principal, which is the initial amount of money, or capital, that we have. Savings are the basis for our principal. We multiply that principal by an amount equal to the rate of return on our investments raised to the number of years over which we are investing. The result of multiplying these two phrases together gets us to the left-hand side of the equation: future value. Future value is the answer to questions such as: if I start with $10,000 and invest at a 10% rate of return for 10 years, how much will I end up with?

The compounding effect, in particular, is the phenomenon of earning profits on our profits. Say a particular $100 investment yields $5 in profit at the end of a year. Going into the next year, we can invest the full $105 and, at the same rate of return (5% in this case), end Year 2 with $110.25 (or a $5.25 profit, $0.25 or a full 5% higher than was earned in Year 1). By year 15, we are earning almost $10 per year in profits from this investment strategy, roughly double what we earned in Year 1.

	Capital at Beginning of Year (A)	Annual Profit % (B)	Annual Profit ($) (A*B = C)	Capital at End of Year (A+C)	Total Profit Since Year 1
Year 1	$ 100	5.0%	$ 5.00	$ 105.00	$ 5.00
Year 2	$ 105.00	5.0%	$ 5.25	$ 110.25	$ 10.25
Year 15	$ 197.99	5.0%	$ 9.90	$ 207.89	$ 107.89

Figure 1.2: Returns compounded over two and 15 years.

Note that time is a key variable in the compound interest formula. For a given rate of return (r) and a certain amount of starting capital (P), then the longer the time horizon we invest over (i.e., a larger "T"), our capital will grow exponentially more. Using the above example, consider the investor starting out with $100, with a 5% expected rate of return. If that person invests their capital for five years, they will end up with $127.63, for a profit of $27.63 ($127.63 - $100). However, if the investment horizon is doubled to 10 years, the investor's portfolio will be worth $162.89, for a profit of $62.89. So, even though we only doubled the time horizon (2x), our profits have actually grown by 2.3x ($62.89/$27.63). That's a powerful result.

	Beginning of Year Capital (A)	Annual Profit % (B)	Annual Profit ($) (A*B = C)	End of Year Capital (A+C)	Total Profit Since Year 1
Year 1	$ 100	5.0%	$ 5.00	$ 105.00	$ 5.00
Year 2	$ 105.00	5.0%	$ 5.25	$ 110.25	$ 10.25
Year 3	$ 110.25	5.0%	$ 5.51	$ 115.76	$ 15.76
Year 4	$ 115.76	5.0%	$ 5.79	$ 121.55	$ 21.55
Year 5	$ 121.55	5.0%	$ 6.08	$ 127.63	$ 27.63
Year 6	$ 127.63	5.0%	$ 6.38	$ 134.01	$ 34.01
Year 7	$ 134.01	5.0%	$ 6.70	$ 140.71	$ 40.71
Year 8	$ 140.71	5.0%	$ 7.04	$ 147.75	$ 47.75
Year 9	$ 147.75	5.0%	$ 7.39	$ 155.13	$ 55.13
Year 10	$ 155.13	5.0%	$ 7.76	$ 162.89	$ 62.89

Figure 1.3: Returns compounded over 10 years.

Compare what we have just described to a job picking apples that pays $10/hour. If we double the amount of time we spend picking apples, from 40 hours to 80 hours per week, for example, then our earnings will only double, along with our increased time allocation. We go from $400/week to $800/week, but we have to work twice as long. Clearly, it is better to let our money go to work for us, to get the benefit of compound interest (2.3x growth in investment profits vs. 2x growth in wages for our apple picker, who had to double their time working). Unless you really like apples (in which case, I'd still advocate finding an undervalued apple company to invest in! Especially if they've just invented the iPhone).

The chart below shows what it looks like for a $10,000 investment to grow over time, according to our compound interest principles. The different lines correspond to different levels of investment returns. For example, the investor who earns 1% annually sees only a very slight change in their $10,000 principal across the 20-year time horizon, while the investor earning a 10% annual return winds up with more than $60,000 by the end of 20 years.

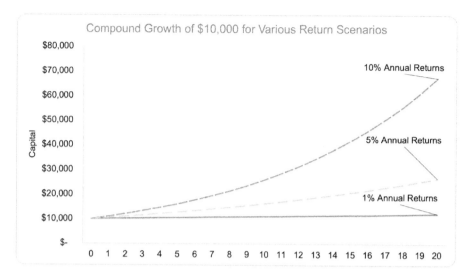

Figure 1.4 Returns compounded over time.

The exponential effect of compounding is one of the main reasons why investors should try to start early. But those benefits certainly don't mean there's no hope for those who haven't exited their 20s with a sizable investment portfolio. Rather, the compounding effect provides the rationale for why setting aside that extra $100 a month can make a big difference over time. Those in the later stages of their careers can still jumpstart their retirement savings by getting the ball rolling and becoming smarter investors, to boost the return profile of their portfolios.

In fact, these days, as the traditional 9-to-5 job with a pension gives way to a much more fluid labor market, the ability to work past the age of 65 could provide people who need to play a little financial catch-up later on in life with an interesting opportunity. The more mature years often see a significantly reduced level of expenses (i.e., the kids have moved out and the house is paid off). This can act as a supercharger for retirement savings and provide some more of that aforementioned financial rocket fuel.

The Dual-Track Lifestyle (Passion Plus Personal Finance)

One way to conceptualize long-term wealth creation and financial independence might be to consider yourself as having two primary professional functions: (1) your day job and (2) your side hustle as a savvy capital allocator. This is the dual-track lifestyle. Working hard at the day job is a great way to advance toward success and fulfillment, but it might not make you wealthy. On the other hand, without a primary way to make money, there would be nothing to generate savings or investment opportunities. At a deeper level, without a passion or fulfillment in day-to-day life, having money isn't going to mean much in the long term. Actively managing one's personal finances should never distract from the real goal of living life to the fullest, but ideally, anxiety about money and feeling a lack of control shouldn't stand in the way, either.

Metaphorically, the day job is what allows us to go buy groceries. The side hustle as a savvy capital allocator is what allows us to turn those groceries into a delicious meal. The neighbors can keep their frozen TV dinners. We are having chicken Marsala with some extra wine on the side (and it didn't cost us any more).

In fact, we can approach our investing side hustle as one might approach learning to cook. Just as someone who wants to eat better or (like myself) just enjoys food might teach themselves to cook over time, we can incrementally optimize our personal wealth creation machine by reading, talking to other investors, seeing how the pros do it, and experimenting in the kitchen with a sourdough loaf in the oven and CNBC on the TV screen.

Now that we've investigated some of the theory behind our basic investment framework, we can move on to self-exploration Phase 1: Know the Numbers, where we take a snapshot of our current financial profile.

PHASE 1

KNOW THE NUMBERS

You have to know accounting. It's the language of practical business life. It was a very useful thing to deliver to civilization. I've heard it came to civilization through Venice which of course was once the great commercial power in the Mediterranean. Double entry bookkeeping was a hell of an invention.

Charlie Munger, Vice Chairman, Berkshire Hathaway

Our financial journey starts with a fact-finding mission. In Phase 1: Know the Numbers, the goal is to build a complete financial profile, showing income, expenses, assets, and liabilities. This information forms the basis of everything we do in subsequent phases and sections, so we need to take the time here to get a look at our numbers. First, we'll gather data relating to our personal finances, a relatively straightforward exercise that mainly involves logging into online bank accounts and investment portals. Then, we'll apply simple accounting and analysis to this data to generate a personal income statement, a balance sheet, and some basic financial metrics. That part of Phase 1 is more extensive.

At least anecdotally, it seems as if a lot of people who strive to improve their financial position jump right into strategies from what I call Phase 2 (saving) or Phase 3 (investing), and skip the Know the Numbers Phase. So, I want to stress that Phase 1 is critical. Jumping right into strategies for saving more or boosting investment returns would be like trying to learn how to race a car without first knowing which car you were in, whether it was an automatic or standard shift, or even if the tank had gas in it, let alone what road you were on! Investing won't be nearly as effective over the long term unless we first understand our basic financial position. So, sharpen those pencils and replace the batteries in that TI-83 calculator you stashed in the attic after high school. Let's get started.

Taking Stock of Our Finances

To start, the reader will want to take a few minutes to familiarize themselves with the key sources of data for their financial profile. This is simpler than it seems. Here's a quick list:

- Bank accounts: checking accounts, savings accounts, and credit cards
- Investment accounts: 401(k)s, IRAs, personal brokerage accounts, life insurance, other investment accounts
- Accounts related to outstanding debts: auto loans, mortgages, student loans, etc.
- Any other seemingly important sources or uses of cash

We'll go over what to do with this agglomeration of databases in a moment, but we need to have them handy. Don't worry if everything isn't pinned down just yet. A financial profile is a living, breathing thing, so there will always be opportunities to make adjustments.

In today's digital world, there are plenty of helpful tools to make compiling personal financial data quick and easy. Most banks today have an online portal that allows users to view their historical bank and credit card statements, as well as current account balances, for example. The statements will give you a sense of how much money is coming in and out of your accounts each month. Similarly, investment accounts and debt providers typically also offer monthly statements and account activity. Pulling the information together might be a bit of an effort at first, but it's relatively straightforward. Then, once the pieces are in place, checking and updating the information will be much easier.

Online tools can go a step further. Many online bank portals will go ahead and categorize your spending for you automatically, based on the bank's algorithms. This groups transactions and balances in a useful format that can be downloaded right to a spreadsheet. It's quick and can be updated any time.

Personal finance applications make this even simpler. Instead of writing everything down on a legal pad, or typing it into a static document online, savvy saver-investors can explore apps such as (at the time of writing) Mint, by Intuit, and Personal Capital, by Empower, which let users import financial accounts into their hub and then pull all that financial data together into helpful dashboards. The apps also let you customize budgets and categorize spending to fit your needs. As time goes on, I suspect that more of these options will be available to the everyday saver. Personal finance websites such as Nerdwallet can be useful to explore, as well.

Bank and investment accounts should each show total cash balances, total investment account balances, and total debt outstanding. All of these should be noted as part of the personal financial profile. Also, we need accurate numbers for income and expenses. On the income side, a most recent tax return or a pay stub should show the annual or most recent monthly income. Gig workers using a platform such as Uber may be able to pull income data directly through the platform's portal. Otherwise, adding up total deposits into one's bank account should give a decent approximation of total income. Bank portals may report this information directly so that it doesn't have to be done manually.

Expenses are a little trickier but a handy start would be to look at the last few months of credit card bills or bank account statements. The quick and dirty method of estimating expenses is to take total withdrawals from checking accounts and to add credit card purchases and rent payments. If rent payments are made from a checking account, they shouldn't be double counted. Likewise, if checking accounts are used to pay for past credit card spending, we don't want to double count this expense. Cash purchases can be estimated by adding up ATM withdrawals from checking accounts (much easier when utilizing either Mint or Personal Capital).

Checklists can be a handy way to keep track of different data sources without having to rediscover them each time you want to update your financial tables. Making a list of all accounts open and their balances can save time down the line.

Compiling this data takes work at first, which is why many times it gets skipped over. But the results are worth it. Once a basic framework is in place for keeping track of income, spending, asset, and liability levels, it should be a relatively low-maintenance exercise to keep the values on an income statement and balance sheet current. Big changes around life events may necessitate a more involved round of updating, but other than that, it is likely that little tweaks here and there will be all that's required.

Putting Our Accounting Pants On

Right around the time that Columbus was busy sailing across the Atlantic Ocean, an equally if not more significant discovery was transpiring in Italy. In 1494, Italian monk Luca Pacioli published *Summa de Arithmetica, Geometria, Proportioni et Proportionalita* (a catchy title to say the least), a work that introduced the concept of double-entry bookkeeping—the bedrock of modern accounting.[8]

Although bookkeeping systems had been in use for some time even before 1494, the introduction of double-entry bookkeeping allowed business owners, investors, and others to develop a more concise and complete picture of a company's financial health, something that became increasingly important over the next several hundred years, as companies transformed into larger collective organizations with multiple stakeholder groups and layers of complexity.

Accounting can have the unfortunate stigma attached to it of being too dense or boring to be worthwhile learning for non-accountants, but hopefully this chapter will generate some enthusiasm by conveying what accounting is and why it is useful. Accounting is just a system for keeping track of financial information by grouping similar categories of transactions and monetary accounts together and doing basic arithmetic on those groupings. This discussion of accounting focuses on a few simple need-to-know concepts that are oriented toward allowing us to take full control of the Three Phases of Wealth Creation, as will be seen.

Many of the definitions and concepts in accounting are traditionally presented with a commercial organization in mind. As a result, a lot of accounting information is presented from the point of view of a company or business. This makes sense, as the majority of accountants are working

---

[8] Investopedia: "Evolution of Accounting and Accounting Terminology."

for and with businesses. Accounting itself is viewed as the language of business. Accounting concepts for individuals, though, with the goal of better understanding their financial profile, form a slightly different set of circumstances. In this realm, we may not have to know the differences between things like accrual and cash accounting, how judgement calls influence depreciation schedules, or how accounts receivable and accounts payable are compiled (if this sounds like Greek would sound to those not fluent in Greek, don't worry—that's exactly why we are skipping over such things). These more advanced topics can be pushed aside while we focus on a few basic financial tables using the information we gathered earlier.

The Two Basic Financial Statements

When I talk about "building a financial profile," I mean that we can organize the different data points of our financial lives into a highly functional framework that is simple to read. For the purposes of this book, that framework will take the form of two financial tables: the Income Statement and the Balance Sheet. More in-depth students of accounting will notice that there is no mention of a Cash Flow Statement here. That is deliberate. We're going to keep it simple.

By assembling an Income Statement and Balance sheet, we should be able to answer questions like:

"What is my annual income?"

"How much do I spend every month on average and where is the money going?"

"Am I saving money every month, or eating into my reserves?"

"What is my net worth?"

"How much leverage (or debt) have I taken on?"

"When can I afford to buy a house instead of renting?"

"Why did I spend so much money on artisanal cheeses?"

Without a basic Income Statement and Balance Sheet, these questions are a lot harder to answer (the answer to the cheese question is easy: they are delicious).

Income Statements

Income statements are sometimes referred to as profit and loss statements (P&Ls). They give an overview of how much money is coming in the front door during a specific time frame ("revenue" or "post-tax income"), how much money is walking out the back door ("expenses"), and how much is staying put in the house ("earnings" or "net income").

A simple income statement might look like what is shown below for Maria, a fictional marketing manager who spends some of her free time driving for Uber (5 stars for Maria!). Take a minute to look it over, but don't worry too much about the specifics for now.

Maria's Sample Income Statement				
	2022	2021	2020	Notes
Revenue:				
Annual Salary	$50,000	$50,000	$50,000	Salary from marketing job
Side Hustles	$2,000	$1,000	$1,500	Money from Uber driving
Income Taxes	-$18,200	-$17,850	-$18,025	35% tax rate
Post-Tax Income (A)	**$33,800**	**$33,150**	**$33,475**	
Expenses:				
Housing costs	$12,000	$12,000	$12,000	Apartment in the city
Utilities	$750	$650	$700	Includes gas, electric & internet
Necessary Food and Beverage Costs	$4,000	$3,500	$3,800	Basic, everyday meals
Discretionary Food and Beverage Costs	$2,000	$1,800	$1,900	Restaurants and bars
Car Payment	$3,000	$3,000	$3,000	Annual payment on car loan
Miscellaneous	$1,000	$1,000	$1,000	
Total Expenses (B)	**$22,750**	**$21,950**	**$22,400**	
Earnings or Net Income (Savings) (A-B)	**$11,050**	**$11,200**	**$11,075**	
Savings Rate (as a % of post-tax income)	33%	34%	33%	

Figure 2.1: Maria's income statement.

The Income Statement separates what we earn (net of what we have to pay to Uncle Sam in taxes) from what we spend that money on. This leaves us with the "bottom line" result of what our net savings or net expenditure is. We've chosen to look at Maria's past three years (2020–2022) of financial data here, but the Income Statement could also be looked at monthly (or even weekly), depending on the situation.

1. Revenue and Taxes: The first section in the Income Statement deals with our revenue and how much we pay in taxes on that money. For someone with a stable, salaried job, this part should be relatively straightforward. The revenue line would equal the total annual salary for that person (Maria makes $50,000 per year as a marketing manager). Freelancers and people with multiple jobs will have a more complicated revenue picture (all the more reason to get in the habit of putting together an Income Statement). As mentioned, Maria is also an Uber driver and earns an extra few thousand dollars per year from her side hustle.

A creative approach to building revenue sources is a helpful mindset to have. Having multiple channels through which money comes in the door makes the overall financial structure more resilient to changes to any of the individual income streams. In other words, even if you aren't running a start-up, it is helpful to think creatively about being an entrepreneur in your own life. Our discussions in Phase 2 will shed more light on the role of entrepreneurship, but a good place to start is to think about certain skillsets or experiences that one has, the unique goods or services they could supply to the market, or areas of market demand that are growing and don't require much capital to pursue.

As most people know all too well, our total (sometimes referred to as "gross") income isn't completely representative of the amount of money coming in the door, because we have to pay taxes. We've assumed a 35% tax rate here and deducted that to arrive at post-tax income, which came out to $33,800 in 2022. This is a "quick and dirty" way to treat taxes and doesn't get into the intricacies of things like itemized tax deductions (such as mortgage interest, for example). Those are important! Taxes are covered in greater detail in Part 2. But overall, using short heuristics like a 35% tax rate on income is a good enough approach and should allow us to plan effectively. (Throughout this Phase, if you can't get down to an exact number with multiple decimal points, don't sweat it. It's okay to approximate numbers, as long as we aren't too far off (+/- 10%)). If using a most recent pay stub or tax return as the basis of a revenue calculation, you likely already took taxes into account and so don't have worry about this step.

Post-tax income is the total amount of funds available to be spent in our day-to-day lives and is one of the two key determinants underlying how much we save per year (with the other part coming up next).

2. Expenses: True to its name, the Expenses section of the Income Statement lists each category of cost. For most people, the big expense categories would include housing (rent or homeowners' expenses), food and beverage, and transportation (payments on a car loan or lease, gas, insurance, monthly public transportation expenses, etc.).

Maria's greatest expense is housing, for which she spends $12,000 per year. This is followed by everyday food and beverage costs, her car payment, and discretionary food and beverage costs. The difference between necessary and discretionary food and beverage costs is that necessary costs are just the basics needed to survive (i.e., going to the grocery store and cooking meals or getting casual meals out), while discretionary expenditures represent those weekend trips out to a sit-down restaurant or having a few drinks at the new disco-themed night club on Eighth Street (I hear the DJ there really knows how to get the people rockin').

It can be daunting to try to keep track of every little cost item, as expenses can vary significantly from month to month (relative to income, which tends to be more stable). This is one reason why I advocate for using some of the online tools—either those offered by banks themselves or by third parties such as Mint. Many times, these applications give a summary view of total expenditures over the past month or year as well as category breakdowns of spending. Manual expense tracking is easily avoided in that case. More detail will be shared here in Phase 2. Either way, having an accurate view on the expense side is critical.

3. Net Income: The goal of the Income Statement is to tally up income and expenses and see what we are ultimately saving or spending each year. Hence, once we are done adding up revenues (net of taxes) and accounting for our different expense items, we take the difference between the two as our Net Income, or Earnings.

One handy thing to calculate after deriving net income is the savings rate, which is arrived at by dividing net income by post-tax income. Maria is a good saver. Her percentage savings rate for 2022 is high, at 33% (i.e., $11,050/$33,800).

Income Statement vs. Budget:

Readers might wonder why I've presented an income statement rather than a budget. There's a reason for that. I emphasize thinking about personal finances from an income statement approach, because it puts more focus on revenue, whereas a typical budget tends to focus primarily on expense categories and cost cutting. One of the key conclusions of this book is that over the long term, focusing on revenue-generating strategies is a winning formula, while over the short-term, cutting costs can have a meaningful, but proportionately lower, long-term impact on the bottom line.

Based on my past interactions, it seems as if most people who are stressing about their personal finances or trying to come up with ways to improve their position start with looking at costs and finding areas to decrease spending (cutting down on restaurant visits, delaying vacations, refusing to buy new socks). While living within one's means and taking a prudent approach to the cost side of things is crucial, I don't think it makes sense to miss the forest for the trees so to speak, and to stress about small costs at the expense of achieving long-term revenue growth. There is only so much time one can devote to their personal finances, and those efforts should go towards strategies that fully maximize wealth creation.

This conclusion mainly comes down to return on effort: that is, is it better to spend time worrying about keeping costs at the absolute minimum, or are we better off looking at ways to grow revenue by increasing our long-term earnings potential? Most of the time, I think the latter is probably the best route, as long as costs aren't excessively high (that is, we start off with a prudent mindset about expenditures). A relatively robust cost-cutting program might yield a few hundred dollars a month in savings. While substantial in its own right, that is nothing compared to the growth in earnings potential over the long-term for someone who gets a strong education, works hard, and positions themself to be a high earner. The cash flow impact there could easily be greater than $50,000 per year, multiples of what one could cut out of their cost structure.

Over the long term, endeavoring to boost one's value-add and set of skills is likely to be a much higher-return effort than trying to just cut costs everywhere and stressing about spending levels. This point can't be emphasized enough. I totally advocate for keeping tight control over one's expenses, but remember that cutting costs isn't going to make you wealthy. This concept will play a greater role in Phase 2. For now, let's move on to the balance sheet.

Balance Sheets

A balance sheet is like a snapshot of your finances at a certain point in time. It's the second key financial table that we are going to create. The income statement lays out income and expense flows, and describes how much we are saving for a given period. The balance sheet identifies the resources that we have at our disposal ("Assets"), the debts and other liabilities that we owe to third parties ("Liabilities"), and the all-important residual value that is left over afterwards ("Equity" or "Net Worth"), at a specific point in time.

Maria's sample balance sheet is shown below. Notice the separation of assets, liabilities, and equity. Also notice how Maria is crushing it in the investment department, with a $100,000 portfolio after setting aside some cash in her checking and savings accounts. This is foreshadowing for our later discussion of the Three Heroes of Capital Allocation, in Phase 3.

Maria's Sample Balance Sheet

Assets:	12/31/2022	12/31/2021
Financial Accounts:		
Checking Accounts	$10,000	$8,000
Savings Accounts	$50,000	$35,000
Investment Accounts	$100,000	$75,000
Physical and Other Assets:		
Home	$300,000	$280,000
Car	$20,000	$24,000
Total Assets (A)	**$480,000**	**$422,000**
Liabilities:	12/31/2022	12/31/2021
Debt/Financial Liabilities:		
Mortgage	$250,000	$275,000
Car Loan	$17,000	$19,000
Student Loan Debt	$20,000	$23,000
Credit Card Debt	$1,000	$1,000
Other Liabilities:		
Unpaid Medical Bills	$500	$0
Total Liabilities (B)	**$288,500**	**$318,000**
Equity or Net Worth (A-B)	**$191,500**	**$104,000**

Figure 2.2: Maria's balance sheet.

As we did with the income statement, we can break the balance sheet up into its constituent parts and tackle them one by one.

1. Assets: These are the resources that we have and control. For most people, assets are going to be made up of (i) financial accounts and (ii) physical and other assets.

Financial accounts are where our cash and investments are stored. They include basic checking accounts, savings accounts, and investment accounts. In addition to a personal brokerage account, investment accounts would also include retirement accounts such as 401(k)s, IRAs, or various insurance products (annuities, life insurance policies, etc.).

Physical and other assets encompass all nonfinancial assets, the largest of which is typically a house, car, boat, or something similar. These are nonfinancial in nature in the sense that there isn't an immediate dollar amount attached to them and they most likely represent a physical thing you can touch. Other large possessions of value would be included here (priceless artifacts buried under Grandma's cherry tree?). We would typically account for physical and other assets at their estimated market value as of the time you were compiling your balance sheet, meaning that if you bought a house for $100,000 15 years ago and it had a market value of $200,000 today, then you would account for it at $200,000 in your personal balance sheet. Likewise, if you bought a car for $30,000 five years ago, it would typically be worth substantially less than that today (maybe $10,000) and so should be included at the newer (lower) amount.

Within the financial accounts and physical asset categories, a good practice is to rank assets by order of liquidity, with the most liquid assets being listed first. Liquidity is a measure of how quickly assets can be converted to cash—the most liquid asset is cash itself. Overall, financial accounts are the most liquid assets that we own, in that it is relatively easy to convert them to cash and move them around as necessary.

On Maria's balance sheet (Fig. 2.2), financial assets are equal to $160,000 (that is, $10,000 + $50,000 + $100,000), while nonfinancial assets are equal to an estimated $320,000 ($300,000 + $20,000). Thus, the total assets equal $480,000 ($160,00 + $320,000).

2. Liabilities: The liabilities section of the balance sheet enumerates all categories of debt and other IOUs that one is responsible for. Similar to the breakout of our assets between financial accounts and other/nonfinancial assets, we can organize liabilities by financial liabilities (i.e., debt) and nonfinancial liabilities.

Part 2 provides a much broader description of debt than we'll go into here, but for now, let's just say that most people come in contact with at least some form of debt in their lifetime. The most common categories are mortgage debt (to finance a home purchase), student loan debt (to finance higher education costs), car loans, and credit card debt. Each debt category has a different set of characteristics relating to the interest rate, amortization (amount of principal that must be paid down each month), maturity date, and secured status (whether or not the lender has a claim on any specific assets of yours). As we shall see, the presence of debt may be a good or bad thing, depending on the reason for borrowing.

Next, the nonfinancial liabilities category would include all other liabilities outside of debt. Mostly this would relate to unpaid bills (unpaid parking tickets, medical bills, annual subscriptions that you have been using but haven't paid for yet, etc.) but could include other special items, as well. Maria has one unpaid medical bill of $500 that would be counted here.

In Figure 2.2 above, Maria's financial liabilities come out to $288,000 (that is, $250,000 + $17,000 + $20,000 + $1,000), while her nonfinancial liabilities, which consist of the unpaid medical bill, are $500. Thus, her total liabilities equal $288,500.

3. Equity or Net Worth: After tallying up the total assets and total liabilities, we can calculate the difference between these two numbers to arrive at "net worth" (also called "equity"). Maria has a solid net worth to grow from, equal to $191,500 ($480,000 - $288,500).

Net worth represents our nest egg, which is the amount of assets we would have left over if, theoretically, we paid off all our debts and other liabilities today. Maximizing net worth is the goal of saving and investing. Simply put, this is accomplished by increasing the value of total assets relative to total liabilities (either the assets have to go up, or the liabilities have to go down). This is a very important concept, because net worth is the basis of wealth, and utilizing a strong savings and investment program to grow net worth over time should result in an improved standard of living. The faster we can grow it, the faster we are enhancing our financial independence.

The Hidden Asset Is You!

I promised at the outset not to make any sensationalist statements such as "the hidden asset is you," but grant me this one exception. After going through the asset and liability calculations above, many people arrive at a negative value for net worth. In short, their total assets are less than the amount of their total liabilities. A lot of people who have graduated college recently and have student debt, for example, are likely to fall into the negative net worth category, which can be a scary thing to face.

However, those calculations left out a very important asset called human capital.

Quick, take a selfie.

The person staring back at you from the camera is your human capital, an asset that represents the value today of all your future wages. The reason human capital doesn't appear on the balance sheet is that it is very hard to estimate. Who can predict what their earnings trajectory will look like over even the next 5 to 10 years, let alone 20 to 40?

But just because it is hard to estimate doesn't make human capital any less important. To the contrary, for people just starting out in their career, human capital is very likely to represent their single largest asset. Developing human capital is the incentive to take out student loans and pursue some form of higher education, in the first place.

As people move through their careers, the trick to building long-term wealth is to maximize human capital (earnings potential) and then to convert that potential into real, tangible, cash savings over time. This, combined with a strong investment program, will do wonders for flipping that negative balance sheet net worth into a highly positive value.

Now, friends, on to Phase 2: Supercharge Savings.

Toolkit Summary—Phase 1

- Gather financial data from various accounts: bank portals, credit and debit card statements, pay stubs, tax returns, statements from debt providers, and investment accounts.
- Build the Income Statement: Revenue – Expenses = Net Income.
- List items by time period (monthly, quarterly, yearly).
- Break out all revenue sources (primary jobs and side hustles). Remember to account for taxes.
- List the large expense categories. Be as granular as you want, but try to at least include the main three to five categories of spending.
- Build the Balance Sheet: Assets – Liabilities = Net Worth.
- Sort items by order of liquidity (how easily they are converted to cash).
- On the asset side, include both financial (cash in checking and savings accounts, investments in stocks and bonds, life insurance policies, etc) and nonfinancial (house, car, rare collection of 80's-themed tchotchkes). For nonfinancial assets, account for them at market value—or what they could be sold for today.
- For liabilities, account for all debts based on total amount owed (perhaps make a note of the time period over which the debt has to be paid). Don't include expenses that haven't been incurred (if you are planning a large vacation next year, for example, this is not a liability yet). Remember to include other liabilities, such as unpaid parking tickets or medical bills.
- Store these in a central location that can be easily accessed and updated. Or, use an app like Mint or Personal Finance to automate most of this upkeep.

PHASE 2

SUPERCHARGE SAVINGS

If you would be wealthy, think of saving as well as getting.
Benjamin Franklin, *The Way to Wealth*

As an elementary school student, I discovered the joys of Halloween candy (I was not the only adolescent who shared this epiphany). However, instead of devouring my favorite Butterfinger, Kit Kat, or Crunch bars, I would fastidiously sort my sugary hoard and lock it in a container for safekeeping. This way, I was assured of having a tasty treat whenever I wished, during non-Halloween months. Once, this practice had an unfortunate, unintended consequence. After I had contracted the flu, my dad helped himself to an Almond Joy from my stash. He came down with the very same flu several days later! There was no joy from that almond. This is hopefully one of the only ways that saving can be dangerous.

Candy fiascos notwithstanding, learning to save consistently is really just a matter of understanding the flow of cash in and out of a bank account and trying to maximize the money we get to keep. Phase 1 is crucial here because it involves getting organized and developing a clear picture of our personal finances (if this picture causes you to gasp in horror, fear not, and read on). Without doing this, it is very hard to move forward.

Once the all-important income statement and balance sheet are developed, we can advance to the meat and potatoes of this journey: optimizing savings and intelligently investing that savings over a long period of time. Doing so efficiently can increase our standard of living without our needing to work any more hours, and move us closer toward financial independence. Savings are the raw material in our production process. The more savings we have, the more potentially profitable investments we can make.

As we shall see, from my standpoint, saving means using education, creativity, and hard work to maximize revenue, while being thrifty—but not overly austere—on the cost side. This "learn to earn" focus is a bit different from a lot of the personal finance literature out there, which often approaches saving strictly as a budgeting or cost cutting exercise.

Savings accumulation in the *Working Capital* way is akin to how CEOs manage their businesses to maximize cash flow. If one were to tune into an earnings call from the average Fortune 500® company, they would likely hear the CEO spend an inordinate amount of time speaking about how the company grows its cash flow by introducing innovative new products or services, expanding its distribution footprint, and reinvesting back into its core operations. Does cost cutting play into this? Of course. But unless the company is shrinking or has been run inefficiently in the past, cost cutting likely isn't the primary way that leading companies create value and grow cash flow. Individuals should think along these same lines. Smart management teams focus on how to derive the greatest benefit from their spending rather than just trying to spend the least amount possible. Yes, they have teams of accountants watching the budget, just as an individual should keep a keen eye on their expenses. But at the end of the day, management allocates most of their time evaluating ways to spend money on attractive initiatives that will help the enterprise win long-term.

A key concept that plays into our saving discussion is upskilling, or moving up the value chain. This means finding higher-value uses for our time. Adding skills that have a higher economic value relative to our existing skillset means that we can shift our time towards activities that bring in more cash. A kid with a lemonade stand that earns $8/hour selling lemonade might find that after a couple of summers on the front lawn, she understands enough about the lemonade industry to consult with other lemonade startups in the neighborhood about how to grow their business. This new consulting service allows her to earn $15/hour. That's upskilling and moving up the value chain.

Productivity enhancements, or being able to do more with less, play a big role in savings growth. Making 5 cups of lemonade per hour won't earn as much as making 20 cups. That's productivity growth driving higher revenue potential. This same concept helps individuals increase their earnings power.

Even the expense side can be approached with more of a learning mindset. Figuring out how to sew a pair of ripped pants so that you can delay your next purchase of new pants a few months reduces total expenses over time and is grounded in increasing one's skillset. Learning how to perform your own oil change, looking up new recipes to take care of extra food in your fridge, traveling on off-peak days, and substituting goods or services for similar but cheaper alternatives are all examples of cost cutting through entrepreneurial thinking. Good savers are thrifty—they see cash flow optimization as a game. Let's learn how to play.

Wait, Why Do We Need Savings in the First Place? Savings as a Form of Defense and Investment Raw Material

Let's start with a philosophical underpinning. Why do we need savings in the first place? It's a fair question to ask. If I am paying all my bills and expenses today, how come I need to be putting money aside? Wouldn't it be better just to buy more things?

While saving money may seem passive and unexciting to many people, there are myriad reasons why it is not only a crucial underpinning to financial success, but it can be accomplished in a creative and fulfilling way. This might seem somewhat akin to the "eat your vegetables" phase of financial transformation, but man, sometimes with the right recipe that broccoli tastes delicious!

Overall, the three principal factors we can look to as driving the need for savings are (i) to provide a cushion for revenue and expense volatility, (ii) to fund large purchases and goals that will come up down the line, and (iii) to passively increase personal wealth through investing (increasing one's standard of living). All three are very important.

Here's a short story to help us tackle the concept of revenue volatility. One day, you walk into work, trip on a bump in the rug, and spill a cup of hot chocolate on your leg. Seconds later, your boss schedules a 6 p.m. meeting to discuss new firmwide font choices. You've had it! It's the last straw in a series of stressful and nonproductive happenings in the workplace. You quit. Losing that income means that you won't be able to pay for your monthly expenses unless you have savings on which to draw. Savings provide the buffer (notwithstanding unemployment insurance, which doesn't apply if you quit) for you to take time off, find a new job, or just more generally ride out the ups and downs associated with a career.

Similarly, adding to cash flow volatility, surprise expenses can pop up from time to time in the form of unexpected medical bills, a faulty ignition in your car or, more positively, a sudden decision to take that trip to Tahiti that you've always talked about. A lack of savings can turn a relatively small change in expense or income into a very large problem.

As for the second reason, most people will need to plan for some key long-term expenses. Typically, the biggest example is retirement. At some point, many of us will stop working for good, and we'll need to be able to fund that loss of income for extended periods of time (I don't necessarily advocate completely stopping work, but that is a conversation for another time). Other large-scale, long-term expenses might include buying a house or new car, planning a vacation, hosting a wedding, starting a business, or funding a child's college education.

Finally, savings are the raw material that allows us to build long-term wealth through investing (and thereby to gradually raise our standard of living). The concept of passively increasing one's standard of living through saving and investing comes up repeatedly throughout this book and is one of the key benefits of wealth creation that savvy capital allocators strive for. The reason is simple: If you can earn $10 an hour working, but investing your money can also earn you the equivalent of $10 an hour, then you can either cut your work hours while maintaining the same income or keep working the same hours and effectively be making $20 an hour. That's the best kind of raise there is.

Without savings, however, there is nothing to invest. Saving can be fun, but at the end of the day it is the pregame. Investing is the game, and it can be very, very fun.

Savings is Potential Energy

In physics, there is a concept called potential energy, which refers to energy that is stored due to an object's relation to its environment. A classic example is a coiled spring (or the more colloquial Slinky), or a boulder sitting at the top of a hill, waiting to be pushed down. While that Slinky and boulder aren't doing anything very interesting at the moment, they have plenty of potential action, should an external force cause the Slinky to make its move down the stairs or the boulder to roll down the hill.

In many ways, personal savings operate in the same manner as potential energy does, and I think this analogy is helpful to keep in mind. On their own, savings are simply an entry in your bank's database. They don't do much other than sit there, perhaps earning a small amount of interest income. However, despite being low in activity, savings are quite high in the potential energy department, because they can be deployed into enjoyable goods, services, or activities. They're ready to step in on a rainy day. Perhaps most important for the purposes of this book, savings can be put to productive use and invested, converting that potential energy into real, live wealth creation.

The Second Master Formula

With that background in mind, we can move on to Master Formula #2, which is:

Savings = Revenue - Expenses

As the Master Formula suggests, the savings rate can be increased through two channels: (1) growing revenue and/or (2) reducing expenses. Over the long term, revenue growth strategies are likely to be the most effective in speeding up our progress toward financial independence. That said, cost-cutting strategies are a direct and simple way to boost the bottom line.

For the Supercharge Savings phase, we mostly focus on ways to make the income statement look more attractive (fashion accessories not included in this version of the book). Despite this focus on the income statement, I don't mean to imply that the balance sheet doesn't factor into our wealth creation efforts. Instead, for the time being, we are going to treat the balance sheet as a given. In other words, for now, we will assume that the assets and liabilities (including debt) are fixed, and we will work instead on boosting savings.

As we progress into Phase 3 and think more about capital allocation (i.e., what to do with those savings), the different categories of the balance sheet will come into play in a much bigger way. So, for all you balance sheet fanatics out there ("Who, me?"), hang tight.

Revenue

Let's start with revenue. As noted in Phase 1, revenue is the category in our personal income statement that represents all of the income that we earn, or the cash coming in the door.

Every person's financial profile and revenue generation model will look a little bit different (sometimes drastically different), but we should be able to boil the typical models down into three categories:

1) One Core Job: Many people fall into this first category, which involves generating income from one core job (often salaried, but perhaps not). Entrepreneurs who run a single company would fall into this category as well, because their income is dependent on one specific source.

2) Core Satellite: A core satellite revenue model involves a core primary job (that "9 to 5"), augmented with one or more side hustles to generate ancillary income. This type of model is becoming increasingly prevalent. I think it is the sweet spot for people who are good at or enjoy doing one thing but are, at the same time, interested in many other things. It allows them to monetize their primary skill set while experimenting outside the lines in other areas.

3) Freelance: Definitions of this model vary, but a freelancer is typically trying to piece together revenue from multiple sources of income, primarily project-based. The freelancer is quite similar to the entrepreneur; however, the freelancer is distinct in that he or she is typically working on a contract basis for another firm, as opposed to owning a business themselves. Freelancers may transition to being entrepreneurs and business owners (and core revenue earners) over time.

Note that a fourth category exists for people whose primary occupation is something other than work (i.e., students, retirees, stay-at-home parents), which is then augmented with part-time employment. This may be thought of as a core satellite approach, where the core is something other than a job (for example, a student with a job at the library front desk on campus).

As you may recall, our sample Revenue section in Phase 1 introduces Maria, a fictional marketing manager with a side hustle driving for Uber (placing her in the "Core Satellite" camp). Maria earns $50k in revenue from her core job, plus another $2k driving for Uber. Her total revenue, then, is $52k, but remember we must account for income taxes. Deducting income tax leaves Maria with a post-tax income of $33,800, representing the amount of actual cash coming in the door (assuming a flat tax rate, for simplicity).

Maria's Sample Income Statement

	2022	2021	2020	Notes
Revenue:				
Annual Salary	$50,000	$50,000	$50,000	Salary from marketing job
Side Hustles	$2,000	$1,000	$1,500	Money from Uber driving
Income Taxes	-$18,200	-$17,850	-$18,025	35% tax rate
Post-Tax Income (A)	**$33,800**	**$33,150**	**$33,475**	

Figure 3.1: Maria's pretax income, taxes, and post-tax income.

Below, we examine some general strategies to grow revenue streams.

Maximizing Revenue

Soul Searching

As mentioned, over the long haul, strategies that aim to increase revenue are likely to yield substantially more wealth than strategies focused solely on cutting costs and managing one's finances on an austere budget.

The ways in which this book approaches maximizing revenue are all about figuring out what the best return-on-time is for a particular person, based on the combination of what their interests are, what they are good at, and what they can get paid to do.

Figure 3.2: The trifecta of maximizing revenue.

It would be very hard for a person to work hard and succeed at something they really disliked, no matter what the monetary benefit of doing so may be. In the same vein, pursuing a career that one is passionate about without some base level of natural affinity might be a tough road to travel (no matter how hard I try, my 5' 7" frame and lack of jumping ability are most likely going to preclude my playing in the NBA). Finally, figuring out what the market rate is for the skills you are trying to develop (i.e., "what you can get paid to do") is a crucial part of the equation, in trying to maximize revenue.

The good news is that, typically, if you enjoy doing something and are passionate about the subject matter, then working hard or improving in that area often doesn't seem like work at all. Artists paint for fun, as well as for improvement and income. The other good news is that the pool of things that lie outside of what you can do (me playing in the NBA, for example) is going to be vastly smaller than the pool of things that are within your circle of competence to achieve. Hard work and a willingness to learn can open lots of doors.

I advocate spending a fair amount of time thinking about these three factors when choosing a new career, evaluating a current position, or contemplating making a change. One way to approach this might be to make a list of the skills or functions needed for each category and try to piece together where the intersection may be. If I really like to read, am passionate about finance, and historically did well in my math classes, maybe a career as a financial analyst is the way to go!

Starting out with industries and types of things you are passionate about seems like a reasonable approach, rather than picking occupations that pay the most or that you have a natural affinity for (just because you are 6'10" doesn't mean you have to play in the NBA, if you're really into investigative journalism). At the end of the day —assuming a basically functioning job market—happiness should be a primary focus.

Another way to see this concept is that an industry of interest may involve such varied occupations that a person can find work they enjoy doing from multiple different angles. Those passionate about food might find their talents leaving them best suited as chefs, while others shine as restaurant managers, drivers, or food-procurement professionals. Still others could be graphic designers working with food-service clients, or lawyers representing food businesses. The industry is the glue that connects these professionals.

Those who fall into multiple categories might enjoy the core satellite approach. That way, a lawyer can set up a quick website and start taking weekend jobs doing graphic design projects for local restaurants in the area. Multiple birds, multiple stones, so to speak.

Steps to Grow Revenue

Understand What You Bring To The Market

Optimizing revenue means maximizing income to the greatest extent practically possible within one's chosen field. The first strategy to do this is to understand our value proposition. This means understanding what value we can offer to the marketplace by way of our specific set of skills, relationships or experience.

SWOT Team (Strengths, Weaknesses, Opportunities, and Threats)

My junior year of college, I had a phone interview for an internship. This was my first phone interview ever, and I was somewhere between mildly excited and mortified (significantly closer to mortified, if I remember correctly). I botched it. At one point, I was so stumped about a question that I loudly kicked my trash can across the room to create a distraction. The interviewer actually moved on from the question after that, leading me to believe that this might be a legitimate defense mechanism if any of our readers get into a bind.

Suffice to say, I didn't get the job. However, one bright spot of this otherwise embarrassing experience was that I had to reevaluate and refocus my interview strategy going forward, which led me to ponder some key questions about myself. One very common interview question that most of us have had to answer at one point or another is: "What are your strengths and weaknesses?"

Well, what are they?

Analyzing our strengths is critical, because strengths are what we can focus on when choosing a career or deciding between different projects to undertake. Weaknesses are equally important, because they are areas for improvement. This collection of key strengths, on the one hand, and weaknesses that can be improved upon, on the other, is the "value proposition" that you can offer to the marketplace. Strengths and weaknesses can be broadly defined, such as "ability to communicate effectively"; but they can also be more specific, depending on a given industry (i.e., "affinity for identifying authentic pieces of art from fakes").

A differentiated background is often a key strength. If you grew up in a different country from where you currently reside, for example, or lived in a particularly rural or urban atmosphere or have traveled to a far-reaching corner of the galaxy, then you probably have a unique perspective to draw on, relative to others in the marketplace. Use it.

Researching the current market rate for your services is a great next step. Collect your "stats"—education level, years of experience, special skills or attributes that you possess—and compare them to the market rate for people who are similarly equipped. Look around on websites such as Glassdoor, LinkedIn, and Indeed, to get a sense of what others are earning. If it appears that you are being underpaid relative to the market, it could be a good time to check in with your boss about the potential for a raise. For example, if I am a civil engineer with five to seven years of experience, and others in my area with those credentials earn $75,000 per year, then knowing that my salary of $70,000 per year makes me roughly $5,000 underpaid relative to the market is a valuable piece of information.

Over long periods of time, working for even a modestly below-market rate can have a material impact on one's finances. For that civil engineer, maintaining the status quo of being $5,000 underpaid would involve sacrificing $25,000, before taxes, over a five-year period.

If, after going through the discovery process, you conclude that you are underpaid, consider speaking with your boss about this and be prepared to do so with hard data, based on what other similar jobs in your area pay for someone with your level of expertise. The simplest way to revert to market rate is to advocate for yourself in your current role. That doesn't mean barging into your supervisor's office and demanding payment like a Wild West bank robber in 1882, but having a frank conversation about how you can get from A to B never hurts.

If going to your boss doesn't work, it might be time to consider making a change, which brings us to the relationship side of revenue generation: networking.

A Different Kind of High-Speed Network (Hint: No Routers Involved)

Networking has long been described as being more about who you know than what you know. It is a broad term for something that many people do every day without even realizing it. Networking just means communicating with other professionals (even digital connections count), to build meaningful relationships. Networking is a helpful tool in terms of understanding your current value proposition and what else is out there. You never know when a contact will come in handy, either with a new job or business opportunity or with valuable industry context that helps you complete a project more effectively.

My dad is the one who taught me the value of networking. He has worked for many years as a producer for documentary film/TV shows and has frequently leveraged professional relationships to find his next good project. As I got older, I came to realize that through networking he was participating in somewhat of a barter system for information and favors—he would help his colleagues find work and pass along leads when he came across them, and in return, his colleagues would do the same for him. As a student of markets, I have to say this economy functions pretty well!

One important thing that took me a while to realize about networking is that it shouldn't be thought of as a sales job, and it isn't about superficially building a contact list. The real juice in networking comes from creating authentic, value-added connections with professionals in a similar field as ours. A strong professional network might only be a few dozen people, but if those connections lead to job opportunities, thoughtful conversations, or other networks, then that is more than enough.

There is much more to networking out there than we can cover in this book, so let's look at just a few key strategies, mostly focused on taking advantage of existing communities of interest:

1. Network at work: The workplace should be the easiest place in which to network, because most of a person's day-to-day is spent there (wherever that may be), and each connection made is directly applicable to that person's professional field. Since people are constantly changing jobs and moving in and out of companies, the group of contacts you build at your primary job will likely expand over time to other companies in the industry. Grabbing the occasional coffee or stopping by to chat with coworkers can have meaningful long-term benefits in the networking department.

2. Network in professional trade groups: Most industries have some sort of professional society that puts on events or even provides networking tools directly. Look around for one that could be worth joining. If you can't find one, maybe build your own. Networking opportunities are usually top of mind for those joining and participating in these organizations, so they can be fertile ground for making new contacts.

3. Network with classmates: One good thing about an education is that our classmates end up entering a diverse set of industries simultaneously with our own career efforts. Many schools offer directories or other tools and events for alumni to connect with one another, and having a common background from a school is a great icebreaker.

4. Network online: Blogs and social media sites open up whole new channels through which to make professional connections. LinkedIn is a great place to start. Just beware of internet scams when networking online.

5. Network with family: Family is the O.G. network. Parents, siblings, cousins, second cousins, third cousins' sister-in-law who works in the media industry. Bring casserole.

Enhance Your Value Proposition

Just as we need to know the numbers before maximizing our saving and investing, we need to understand our current strengths and value proposition before moving on to optimizing and enhancing them. Over time, those who can enhance their value proposition should be paid for it. In other words, improving what you bring to the dinner table should, on average, translate into more bountiful and better-tasting meals.

This concept is rooted in productivity for businesses because, on average, a worker's wage can only increase over the long-term if they increase their value to their organization (a simplistic explanation for how earnings grow, but a useful one to understand why we focus on enhancing one's value proposition).[9]

To digress for a moment, classical economics employs the principle that in efficient industries (meaning all firms are more or less on the same playing field), no companies are able to earn above-average economic profits over the long-term. In such hypercompetitive markets, companies can't rely on raising prices and therefore must work more productively to increase volume, instead. As labor markets are relatively efficient (some more than others), what this implies for workers is that in order to earn more, by and large, they have to produce more.[10] For example, if Jordan is

---

[9] In this context we are referring to above-inflationary wage increases (i.e., outside of an annual cost-of-living adjustment). Growing wages above inflation over time is the process by which workers move up the economic ladder.

[10] This is the same for entrepreneurs or freelancers, as well as for regular W-2 employees. It does make the assumption that workers are fairly compensated for their labor, however, which doesn't always hold true.

a factory worker producing five units of output per hour in an industry with perfect competition, he'll need to find a way to produce more than five units per hour, in order to increase his wage over long periods of time (all else being equal).

This direct link between productivity and income sometimes gets lost in the job-market noise about salaries, promotions, job titles, and comparisons to other workers. However, I think it is the North Star for making more money in the long run. If someone is bringing greater value and productivity to the table, either their current employer is forced to pay them more, or someone else will.

With that in mind, let's look at some ways to increase productivity over both short and long time frames.

Door Number 1: Work Harder

This is a bit of a tongue-in-cheek introduction to enhancing one's value proposition. That said, it certainly seems reasonable to say that the quickest way to boost your value proposition is to increase the amount of effort you allocate to your job. Leaning on our factory worker example, if Jordan can produce five units of output per hour by spending 30 minutes actually working and 30 minutes posting sepia-toned pictures of the factory on his blog, then working for the full hour should lead to increased productivity. Wage gains will most likely follow.

Working hard is certainly a prerequisite to long-term monetary success. There will always be examples of lottery winners who stumble into millions, but that is the exception and not the norm. Eating spinach and rolling up the sleeves is ground zero for improving outcomes.

Door Number 2: Work Smarter

Seemingly in direct opposition to Door Number 1, our second strategy is to take a page out of the book of laziness and to find ways of increasing productivity without increasing our physical or mental exertion. Sure, it might be satisfying to carry water up the hill to your house, bucket by bucket, but maybe it would be easier to just live next to the lake and sell your home to someone who puts a premium on expansive, elevated views of the valley. Or, install one of those fancy new pipe systems that bring water up the hill for you, so you can focus on running your virtual travel agency. That's working smarter.

Take Jordan, for example. Perhaps he discovers a new method of completing his tasks at the factory that increases his output from five units per hour to seven. Not only can he use this discovery to enhance his own productivity, but he can likely bring it up to his supervisors, for implementation across the company. Jordan is on his way to the top by working smarter.

Since the dawn of time, working smarter has been the magic elixir behind most productivity gains in the wider economy. After all, there are only so many hours in the day, and so much physical and mental energy present in a person, meaning that working harder can only get you so far. Learning how to be more efficient and do more with less is key to boosting productivity and increasing earnings. Hence, we'll spend a disproportionate amount of time behind Door Number 2.

Smart work manifests itself in a variety of ways, but for our purposes, working smarter involves developing an edge or efficiency in our approach to work and emphasizing learning before, during, and after the proverbial "doing." The gold standard here should be to put in the time during and outside of the workday to learn the foundational skills necessary for your job and to continually add to that skill set over time (with the goal of becoming an expert in your field).

Education and Learning

A formal education is a great way to boost one's ability to work smarter. While we are growing up, learning is front and center because we go to school every day. But after graduation, learning often takes a back seat to "doing." Sure, we learn how to do our current jobs, but that kind of learning may be coincidental to the doing. What we advocate here is a more aggressive form of learning in and around the workplace, with the express goal of increasing knowledge and improving one's value proposition.

This is a hands-on activity and can be accomplished by getting smart about your industry (see below), identifying key skills that are adjacent or external to your current job function and gradually learning them (expanding one's competence set), studying the value creators and thought leaders at your company and in the industry, even researching interesting products or services offered by competitors. Some fields may have certifications relevant to the job, which should be explored. Be curious.

Organization

Learning how to work more efficiently involves organizing time to maximize productivity as well. For example, ditching the Post-It notes for Google Calendar, or outlining each day's goals in the morning before work. Communicating around key milestones with coworkers so that everyone is on the same page is another example. Technology is our friend in terms of improving organizational efficiency. Luckily, there are numerous free tools out there to help us automate basic tasks and repetitive actions in our daily lives (both inside and outside of work).

Be an Analyst in Your Industry

Being an analyst in your industry is also likely to yield strong results and allow one to work smarter. What I mean is that people should make an effort to really understand the context of their job within their respective industry, and of that industry within the broader economy.

Understanding the context of your role and company is key to figuring out where the value-creating opportunities are in the industry and how that industry is likely to fare over time. To put this in perspective, you could have positioned yourself as the best horse-drawn carriage driver in 1903, but it wouldn't have mattered, because that was the year the Ford Motor Company sold their first car, and the carriage industry was decimated by automobiles in the following decades. The industry backdrop matters, and being smart in this area should lead to better long-term prospects for personal wealth creation.

Part of being an analyst in your industry and at your company means assessing the value-add of other job functions, as well. It isn't enough to confine yourself to the sales team and to optimize within that group. You also need to understand product development, marketing, and what the demand drivers are for your company's products or services (and how they are financed). The smarter you are about the industry you are a part of, the easier it will be to uncover ways to add value to your existing organization and to augment your current skill set.

Looking around your organization, you might find that the quickest way to learn about the other components of your company is to volunteer your free time to work on projects with other teams (note: this may not always be possible, but if it is, then it is an opportunity that should definitely be explored, especially for more junior employees). Any slack or downtime could be an opportunity for you to reach out to other teams and see if you can assist on their projects.

Another good place to look for industry context is online. Setting up a Google Alert for companies in your industry and common industry keywords is a great way to passively start putting things in context. Make it a habit to read press releases, interviews, white papers, etc. that your company is involved in to get a sense of the news flow around important changes in the industry.

Taking note of any publicly traded companies in your industry can produce helpful material, as well. Chances are, the leading public companies in your industry will release a fair amount of industry background research and updates for their investor base. Type "{Public Company Name} Investor Relations" into a search engine and take a look at presentations, annual reports (paying particular attention to any annual shareholder letters available), or press releases. This is how investment analysts "get smart" on the companies they follow, and there's no reason that employees or entrepreneurs can't use the same knowledge base to uncover their own value-add opportunities. Creating a watchlist of public companies in Yahoo Finance, Google Finance, or the Stocks app is a great way to consume up-to-date info about relevant companies in your industry. This plays into our discussion on investing later on.

Overall, having this broader, more interdisciplinary view of your job's significance—and that of the industry—will make you better at your current role and likely open up opportunities to move up or laterally (if you find there are better opportunities elsewhere).

Augmentation Opportunities

Doors Number 1 and 2 offer suggestions for boosting output and efficiency within the context of your core job or business opportunity. Increasingly, though, there are new ways to augment revenue outside of the core. These can broadly be described as side hustles and other opportunities.

Side Hustles

Side hustles are anything systematic or repeatable that can be done to earn extra cash outside of a core job. The emphasis here is on repeatable opportunities that can augment current income over time. Side hustles have existed as long as labor markets have been around; however, they have taken on new importance with the advent of technology. Tech has by and large lowered the information and transaction costs for people pursuing side hustles and made an expanding set of income streams available to pursue.

The most prevalent example of the side hustle concept today is probably to drive for Uber or Lyft or to join the flexible workforces of any of the other gig-economy apps (TaskRabbit, DoorDash, etc).[11] The main idea behind side hustles is that they are a flexible and part-time way to earn some extra cash. As with the strategies for core jobs, a good way to approach a side hustle might be to contemplate things that you are good at or enjoy doing and that can add the most value to the marketplace. For example, if you are constantly going to the gym (or as some people would say, "gettin' buff"), maybe consider personal training or hosting a workout class. If you are a CPA and have some free weekend time, maybe look for

---

[11] This is distinct from those who are employed full time by the gig economy, which would sit more in the core revenue model.

small business accounting opportunities. Perhaps your garden and landscaping abilities have approached an expert level since you bought that house in the suburbs, and you can now apply those learnings to the neighbor's forsythia bush in exchange for cash. Always try to leverage or enhance your existing skill set, because these functions are what the marketplace is most likely going to pay you for. Skills drive productivity which drives earnings.

On a very hot day recently, I walked past a basket that was filled with handheld fans. It had a sign that said "Fans: $5. Leave money in the basket." Suffice to say, I'm a fan of this entrepreneurial side hustle. By the looks of it, about half of them had sold by the time I had come across the basket. I really liked how simple and easy the idea was. And talk about product market fit—it was 95 degrees at the time (Fahrenheit for anyone reading from outside the U.S.). The only drawback was that I didn't have $5 on me. If the business proprietor here had included a Venmo account to send money to, they would have had the fan industry in the palm of their hand (alright, enough with the puns, I promise). Side hustles don't have to be huge or produce tens of thousands of dollars of revenue. Micro-entrepreneurship is just as potent.

An exciting opportunity for side hustles is to find something that not only leverages your existing skill set, but enhances it. Slightly adjacent industries, like the CPA pursuing the small business accounting opportunity mentioned above, might be a good example of something that would probably both enhance one's skill set in their core job and provide income on the side.

Opportunities that develop goodwill or new relationships in your community may also create positive externalities and make you more effective in your day-to-day role (this also counts as networking—double points!). Take, for example, a small daycare startup that provides value for families in one's area and also creates a new sense of community and social cohesion for those involved. The good thing about side hustles is that they serve to augment rather than replace your core job, so they can be approached with perhaps a more exploratory or curious mindset, since you aren't solely reliant on them to pay your bills.

Side hustles can be a great creative and entrepreneurial outlet. Keeping a notebook (digital or not) with interesting concepts or ideas to try out as side hustles would be one way to get the wheels turning. Getting in the habit of sitting down with a cup of coffee or tea and hashing out the basic framework of a business plan for some of the more promising ideas could be a fun way to start making progress on side hustles, even if you don't seriously intend to pursue those opportunities yet.

One other concept to think about with side hustles is the level of capital commitment necessary to get rolling. The best side hustles are those that can be initiated without any dollars being spent up front. These so-called "capital light" opportunities allow you to explore things stress-free, with the ability to walk away at any time. As soon as a material amount of capital is needed to jump-start a side hustle, it becomes more of a full-fledged business opportunity, which should likely entail more concrete thinking up front (a business plan, greater time commitment, etc.).

Over time, it's entirely possible that a side hustle could graduate into a core job or business opportunity. Lots of small businesses have sprung up this way, with a person exploring a passion of theirs outside of the workday only to realize that the side hustle provides a real business opportunity. The analogy of this new "full-time" side hustle in the context of our discussion of revenue models might be for an alien satellite to invade earth, replacing the earthly core job with the new, outlandish side hustle. The movie version could be called *Your Side Hustle Attacks*, starring Tom Cruise.

Other

For simplicity, we define this category as a catchall for any singular ways to make a buck. In contrast to side hustles, which are systematic or repeatable small-scale business opportunities, "Other" applies to opportunities that pop up from time to time but otherwise wouldn't be expected to recur. Helping a friend move in exchange for pizza, winning a fantasy football pool, and finding a $10 bill on the sidewalk all sit comfortably in Other.

Just as a side hustle might graduate into a full-fledged core business opportunity over time, activities in the Other category might repeat enough to graduate them into true side hustles. In this way, painting a neighbor's fence for cash once might turn into a weekend painting business when the rest of the neighborhood catches wind of it.

Entrepreneurship in Action

When it comes to enhancing revenue, many of the things we look at involve taking an entrepreneurial mindset towards charting one's career path and enhancing their skillset. The ability to transition to entrepreneurship and launch one's business is a logical outgrowth of that endeavor. Working for someone else means renting your time to their organization for payment. When you own your own business, however, the fruits of your labor are yours.

Put otherwise, if you generate surplus productivity in your job, it should eventually flow into promotions, higher bonuses, or other opportunities to grow revenue. But much of that surplus will also go towards increasing the profitability of your employer. As an entrepreneur and business owner, you get to keep 100% of the productivity you generate, meaning that your upside isn't capped. As a result, searching for opportunities to become the owner of your business is likely to be time well spent.

Toolkit Summary—Revenue Growth Checklist

- The Second Master Formula: Savings = Revenue – Expenses.
- Find the intersection of what you are good at, what you can get paid for, and what you enjoy doing.
- Have a firm grasp on your value proposition —What can you do that no one else can? What are your key areas of strength? What could you be better at?
- Build a powerful network (focus on quality over quantity).
- Move up the value chain.
- Probably work harder, but definitely work smarter.
- Invest in education.
- Learn process improvement techniques and how to be more organizationally efficient. Use the time you free up to invest in education.
- Be an analyst in your industry. Think critically about where the industry is headed and who the breadwinners are going to be.
- Look for side hustles and other augmentation opportunities. Sit down and write sample business plans. Think like an entrepreneur.

Expenses

Cutting expenses is the other side of the coin when it comes to boosting monthly savings. In fact, from a tax perspective, it is a lot more efficient to cut a dollar of expenses than to earn a dollar more of revenue. This is because that extra dollar of revenue has an associated tax bill, so you only get to keep roughly \$0.65 of it (assuming a 35% tax rate), while each dollar of expenses cut flows through 100% to savings.

The idea of cost cutting can seem stressful. After all, doesn't that mean that we now have to go without certain goods, services, or experiences that we may have become accustomed to? That may be true: Depending on one's budget and desired level of savings, some expenditures may have to be pared back. However, in my experience, most of the time, there are often ways to cut costs that don't actually detract from one's happiness. Instead, these expenses are sometimes hardly remembered several months after they've been cut (although the satisfaction from a positive savings impact is remembered fondly). Note that by "budget," we mean all of the expense items outside of income taxes that would show up in a personal income statement.

Cost cutting should instead be viewed as a treasure hunt in which we search for ways to strip out inefficiency and waste from the budget, exposing a cleaner expense profile and freeing up resources to invest or to redeploy into more impactful experiences. Each unnecessary expense item that is found and eliminated translates directly into either more capital to invest or a new, presumably better good or service to consume. Viewed through this lens, it should become clear that the opportunity to cut costs should be a net positive for one's happiness, rather than being a detractor.

Strategies to Lower Expenses

From an effort standpoint, when evaluating costs, it is more efficient to focus the most time on the biggest expense categories. Figuring out how to cut 10% of your housing costs or 20% off your car purchase is going to be significantly more impactful than going without a cup of coffee twice a week. So, a good place to start is to list your top five to seven biggest consumers of cash on a monthly or annual basis.

Luckily, by way of developing the personal income statement in Phase 1, we should already have a list of the various expense categories and how they combine to form our monthly budget. For most people, the largest expense categories are going to be some combination of the following:[12]

1. Housing: This is usually the largest category. Monthly rent plus utilities and insurance, or homeowner's costs to the extent applicable. We discuss homeowner's costs in more detail in the Housing section.

2. Food and beverage: Breakfast, lunch and dinner. Sometimes snacks. Food and beverage costs can be bifurcated into (i) non-discretionary meals and (ii) discretionary meals (or "splurges" if you prefer), like going out to restaurants or bars.

3. Transportation: A catchall for how we get around. Transportation by car (car loan, insurance, lease costs, gas, normal wear and tear, etc.), public transportation (monthly metro card, bus tokens, etc.) or other (ridesharing, new bike, etc.). A line item for average airfare or expenses for larger trips or vacations could also be helpful to include here.

4. Healthcare: Healthcare costs can be complicated to put a finger on because they might include a combination of employer-employee paid insurance premiums, co-payments or co-insurance, or fully out-of-pocket expenses.

5. Shopping/Misc. Travel and Entertainment: This category includes all other shopping (clothes, electronics, other goods, etc.) and travel/entertainment costs not previously categorized. Concerts, movies, and other live events all occupy this category.

---

[12] Childcare expenses are another big cost for many households, although for our purposes I treat them as a subset of all the other expense categories (i.e., childcare costs would span healthcare, housing, food and beverage, etc).

6. Education: For many people, education costs are an increasingly large part of the budget. This could include higher education costs (including student loan payments), private school costs, after-school programs, books and other educational materials, certification courses, etc.

7. Subscriptions: Everything from Internet service, streaming services, phone bills, cable and Amazon Prime to magazines and other media.

This list is by no means exhaustive but should at least suggest the majority of expenses for the majority of people.

The Current, Average, and Target Budgets

The steps for developing a sound budget involve simply figuring out (i) what we are spending today (and on what categories) and (ii) what we would like to spend in the future in order to meet our savings goals. For our purposes, despite a description of the budget and expense items so far as one unified set of costs, it is actually more accurate to think of several separate budgets: the current budget, the average annual budget, and the target budget.

The current and average annual budgets are both representations of point (i): what we are spending on today. Each tells a slightly different story. That's why we look at both, to get the best overall view of our current spending level. The target budget, on the other hand, is a representation of point (ii): what we would like to spend in the future to meet our savings goals. There are a couple of different ways to develop the target budget, as will be seen.

Before we get started, let's introduce Skylar. Skylar is a sales representative for a Fortune 500 firm and has no side hustles currently. She earns $60,000 per year on average (after taxes) but would like to take a closer look at her expenses, because her revenue is tied in part to commissions on sales and so can be volatile. Skylar's expense breakdown for the past two months and for the past two years are as follows:

Skylar's Sample Expense Breakdown	Dec. 2022	Nov. 2022	2022	2021
Rent	$ 1,545	$ 1,545	$ 18,000	$ 17,500
Utilities	$ 45	$ 65	$ 750	$ 750
Student Loan Payment	$ 750	$ 750	$ 9,000	$ 9,000
Necessary Food and Beverage Costs	$ 400	$ 480	$ 5,000	$ 4,300
Discretionary Food and Beverage Costs	$ 165	$ 190	$ 2,000	$ 3,200
Car Payment (incl. gas and insurance)	$ 480	$ 500	$ 5,200	$ 5,000
Travel and Vacation	$ 2,000	$ -	$ 2,000	
Miscellaneous	$ 180	$ 240	$ 2,500	$ 500
Total Expenses (B)	$5,565	$3,770	$44,450	$40,250

Figure 3.3: Skylar's expenses for the past two months and two years.

Let's borrow Skylar's expense breakdown to give us a sense of how the current and the average annual budget are created.

As mentioned, first is the current budget, which is based on current monthly expenses. Multiplying those by 12 gives us the run-rate of expenses to be expected for the coming year, if everything stays the same as in the current month.

Based on Skylar's expense breakdown, we can use December—her most recent month of expenses—to give us a sense of her current budget:

Skylar's Sample Expense Breakdown	Dec. 2022	Multiple to Annualize	Current Budget
Rent	$ 1,545	12.0x	$ 18,540
Utilities	$ 45	12.0x	$ 540
Student Loan Payment	$ 750	12.0x	$ 9,000
Necessary Food and Beverage Costs	$ 400	12.0x	$ 4,800
Discretionary Food and Beverage Costs	$ 165	12.0x	$ 1,980
Car Payment (incl gas and insurance)	$ 480	12.0x	$ 5,760
Travel and Vacation	$ 2,000	12.0x	$ 24,000
Miscellaneous	$ 180	12.0x	$ 2,160
Total Expenses (B)	$5,565		$66,780

Figure 3.4: Skylar's current budget, based on last month's expenses.

Skylar's current budget shows that if, over the next year, her expenses stayed the same as they have this past month, then she can expect to spend roughly $67,000 during that period ($66,780, to be exact). At first, this seems troubling, because Skylar's income is only expected to average $60,000 per year. If her yearly expenses fulfilled the predictions based on her current budget, then she would be burning roughly $7,000 of savings just to keep up with her expenses ($67,000–$60,000).

Taking a closer look, however, we see that Skylar went on vacation in December, which cost her $2,000 (her $2,000 vacation destination will remain her business). Since Skylar's total expense item in 2022 was also equal to $2,000, we can infer that this is the only vacation that she took. Hence, the current budget isn't giving us a great representation of the actual expenses that we can expect Skylar to accumulate over the next year, because we have annualized a big one-time item.

Because of the shortcomings of the current budget, a more useful budget, in our opinion, is the average annual budget, which represents total expenses for the past year. For Skylar, we are viewing her expenses at the end of December, which means that her average annual budget is the same as her total expenses in 2022 If we were looking at this, say, at the end of July, we would be taking the past 12 months (from July through the prior August) as the average annual budget. This is sometimes called the "trailing 12-month" number.

Skylar's Sample Expense Breakdown	2022	Multiple to Annualize	Average Annual Budget
Rent	$ 18,000	1.0x	$ 18,000
Utilities	$ 750	1.0x	$ 750
Student Loan Payment	$ 9,000	1.0x	$ 9,000
Necessary Food and Beverage Costs	$ 5,000	1.0x	$ 5,000
Discretionary Food and Beverage Costs	$ 2,000	1.0x	$ 2,000
Car Payment (incl gas and insurance)	$ 5,200	1.0x	$ 5,200
Travel and Vacation	$ 2,000	1.0x	$ 2,000
Miscellaneous	$ 2,500	1.0x	$ 2,500
Total Expenses (B)	$44,450		$44,450

Figure 3.5: Skylar's average annual budget, based on 2022 expenses.

Hence, based on her trailing 12-month expenses, Skylar's average annual budget is $44,450. If her expense levels stay constant, this is what we'd expect her to spend over the next year. It is quite a bit lower than was implied by her current budget. We can divide the average annual budget by 12, in order to get it into a monthly format. In the foregoing example, this comes out to about $3,700 ($44,450/12). This is the average amount we would expect Skylar to spend in any given month, based on what she's spent over the last year, which is quite a bit less than she spent in December ($5,565). The reason we prefer this approach is because it includes the average value for "lumpy" items such as one-off costs that come up every now and then and may or may not be included in the current monthly budget. Remember, we are trying to solve for average income and expenses over time in order to optimize long-term savings.

The average annual budget would suggest a rosier picture for Skylar's expected savings. With her annual income of $60,000, she could expect to be saving $15,550 ($60,000 - $44,450) over the next year, assuming things stayed the same, for a savings rate of 26% ($15,550/$60,000).

As mentioned at the outset, though, Skylar's income is tied to sales commissions and so can be expected to fluctuate quite a bit year over year. Because of this, she feels she should try to save more of her income than

$15,550/year, and so she turns to our final budget, the target budget, in order to help her get there.

The target budget represents our goal: the level of average monthly or annual expenses that we feel comfortable with and that provides us with an attractive residual level of savings to invest. When most people sit down and try to develop a budget, what they are working toward is the target budget. But how do we go about figuring this out? For our purposes, there are actually two different ways to develop the target budget, and we will discuss both of them below. As we go through this, in the back of your head keep in mind that later on, during the discussion of "Searching For Expense Savings," we will focus on trying to transition from the average budget to the target budget by looking at each large expense category and figuring out where inefficiencies exist (there's that treasure hunt we mentioned).

Developing the Target Budget

There is no single answer in terms of how much a given person should be spending on each expense category. The right target budget depends at least to some extent on a person's age or life-stage, geographic location (higher- vs. lower-cost areas), income level, current level of assets and liabilities, and expected income and expense levels in the future (including goals that need to be saved for, like vacations, college tuition, retirement, etc.).

That said, we need to have some sort of target budget in mind, because it will help us plan and save more consistently and accurately. The thing to remember is that target budgets are fluid and subject to change.

There are two main approaches that we would suggest in developing a target budget. We call them the income-first approach and the expense-first approach. A combination of each approach might yield the best overall representation of a target budget, although individuals may find they prefer one approach to the other.

Income-First Approach

The income-first approach starts with the level of expected revenue and a desired savings rate, and backs into an implied expense level. The idea here is to try to come up with a level of savings that allows for healthy investment and the funding of long-term goals, and so it doesn't matter so much what the "level" of expenses is, as long as we can fund those goals.

For example, say that based on her expected revenue of $60,000, Skylar wants to save 35% in order to ride out any revenue volatility with her commission-based job and put some money away for investments to fund long-term goals. Her desired savings level would then be $21,000 (=$60,000*35%). With revenue of $60,000, a desired savings level of $21,000 would imply that Skylar's annual expenses were $39,000 (=$60,000 - $21,000). Under the income-first approach, this $39,000 of expenses is therefore Skylar's target budget. As a result of the work we did in the last section, we know that during the prior 12-month period, Skylar spent $44,500, or $5,500 more than her target level.

Hence, based on the income approach, Skylar would be looking for ways to strip out $5,500 of cost from her expenses, in order to hit her savings goal. With this information in mind, the next step would be for her to go line item by line item through her list of expenses and look for opportunities to cut back. Discretionary purchases, such as Discretionary Food and Beverage Costs, Travel and Vacation expenses, and whatever is in Miscellaneous, might be good places to start. Remember, too, that this is an iterative process, and also that a bump in Skylar's revenue of $5,500 (after taxes) would accomplish the same dollar amount of savings as cutting costs.

Expense-First Approach

As we saw, the income-first approach to developing a target budget starts with revenue and a desired savings rate in order to back into what the right level of expenses may be. The expense-first approach, on the other hand, starts with each of your budget categories and tries to come up with reasonable expense levels, one by one. If you have ever sat down with a blank sheet of paper and tried to write out your target budget from scratch, you did something very similar to the expense-first approach. The expense-first approach is also similar to something called zero-based budgeting, which comes up frequently in the corporate world. With zero-based budgeting, the goal is to build the necessary expenses for various categories from the ground up each year, in order to start fresh and remove excess spending from the start.

Notice that we are looking for a "reasonable" level of expense for each category. What is reasonable is going to be different for each person, depending on their situation. One way to gauge this is to figure out what other people in similar living situations as yourself are spending on everyday items. What are average rents in the area versus what you are paying? How many times do you go to restaurants compared to how often your friends go? Which streaming services do you really need? Going line item by line item and figuring out a reasonable level for each category should get you to a target budget that is workable for a person in your area. The easiest way to see this in action is probably in the rental housing category, because with services such as Zillow, Apartments.com, etc., one can figure out pretty quickly what market rents for a studio, 1br, 2br, etc., are in a given zip code.

To put the expense-first approach in context, Skylar would be looking at each of her categories as a blank slate (rent, utilities, student loans, etc.) and trying to decide what the minimum or most prudent level of spending for those categories would be. Some categories, such as student loans or housing costs, might not have much flexibility built into them, and so what's reasonable may not be very different from what is currently being paid. As with most budgeting analyses, discretionary spending items are typically going to be the best candidates for cost cuts.

Perhaps, after going through this analysis, Skylar ends up with a target budget of $40,500, based on the expense-first approach:

Skylar's Target Budget - Expense-First Approach		
Rent	$	16,800
Utilities	$	700
Student Loan Payment	$	9,000
Necessary Food and Beverage Costs	$	5,000
Discretionary Food and Beverage Costs	$	1,000
Car Payment (incl. gas and insurance)	$	5,200
Travel and Vacation	$	800
Miscellaneous	$	2,000
Total Expenses (B)		$40,500

Figure 3.6: Skylar's target budget, based on the expense-first approach.

The income-first and expense-first approaches should hopefully end up outputting a similar monthly level of expenditure. In Skylar's case, the income-first analysis implies that she should be spending $39,000, on average, which is very close to what the expense-first approach implies ($40,500). So, Skylar now knows that cutting $4,000 to $5,000 out of her annual expenses is likely to get her to her savings goal, which she could then invest or otherwise put to productive use.

If there are small (<20%) discrepancies between results from the two approaches, don't worry. The target budget is an iterative process, and you may not end up with one magic number to hit. Large differences, however, may signal that we need to go back and evaluate assumptions with greater scrutiny.

What I've presented here in terms of budgets isn't the only way to approach tracking and managing expenses. Even a super simple strategy such as trying to keep daily expenses below a certain threshold such as $40 could be a viable way to think about budgeting. As with many topics in this book, readers should feel comfortable experimenting with different processes to find one that fits their lifestyle and goals.

Searching for Expense Savings, and Why Pizza Still Fits into the Equation

Once we have a rough target budget to compare to our current spending levels, we can look at ways to try and bridge the gap between the two. Getting from A (current expenses) -->B (target expenses) and staying close to B is the end game in terms of monthly budgeting and controlling expenses. As we will see, there is no home-run swing that is going to get us there (although there might be a fair amount of low-hanging fruit, or actions that can be taken that produce a disproportionate reduction in expenses, relative to the cost of doing so). Rather, moving closer to the target budget is an iterative process that involves reviewing an entire cost structure over time and looking for opportunities. A treasure hunt, indeed.

Regardless of the specific strategies outlined, my view is that when it comes to cutting costs, the mindset is most important. Nutritionists point this out in their advice to people trying to lose weight, in that many times it is more about trying to live a healthy lifestyle and being conscious of one's body than following a specific dietary or workout program to a T (i.e., "Don't touch my pizza, I ran today!"). Graduating is more important than getting a perfect score on every test.

A similar concept applies to our financial health when pondering expense reductions: It isn't so much about swearing off restaurants for the next five years. The broader goal is to develop a prudent mindset that reduces one's likelihood to overspend and automatically questions the necessity of big purchases.

That said, a prudent mindset needs to be paired with some sharp tools for cutting costs out of the budget, so we'll explore some basic strategies, starting with the biggest expense categories and working our way down.

Underpinning our discussion on expenses is the goal of shifting costs down and out, meaning that we want to find ways to reduce the amount of cash being spent on the things we buy (down), or delay purchases and ultimately buy fewer things (out). Reducing the cash spent on things we buy might involve looking for substitutes or waiting for more favorable times to purchase.

A classic example of the first point is buying the generic or private-label version of that toothpaste you like rather than the name brand, which costs more. Maintaining the quality of the product or service you buy while trading down to a lower price is actually quite similar to the investment optimization strategies we will discuss in Phase 3 (trying to buy good companies at cheap prices). Shopping at a thrift store or buying used goods instead of new ones incorporates the skillset of having a discerning eye and understanding the quality of the things we buy, a skill that can be honed over time.

An example of waiting for a more favorable market might be delaying the purchase of a new TV until Black Friday deals start popping up in the fall. Alternatively, taking advantage of a decline in interest rates to refinance a house or waiting for a downturn in real estate markets to start a renovation (when construction costs are likely a lot lower) represent examples of buying in favorable markets.

Delaying purchases means shifting our expense structure forward in time, which ultimately leads to us buying fewer things and spending less money. Yes, a new phone would be great, but can we challenge ourselves to get an extra six months out of the one we currently have?

Let's extend our discussion by analyzing the top three monthly expenses: shelter, food, and transportation expenses.

Rent or Homeowner's Expenses (shelter)

Rent or homeowner's costs are often the biggest expense category, consuming on average anywhere from 15% to 25% of disposable income, according to the OECD, although in some instances, housing costs can take up 30% to even 50% of income.[13] Therefore, it makes sense to allocate a big chunk of time to analyzing how these expenses could be reduced. We'll delve deeper into the economics of homeownership in a later chapter, so for now, we'll just focus on rent expense, as a proxy for total shelter costs.

Cutting housing costs can be broken down into two simple strategies: (i) make do with less or (ii) get the same for cheaper.

Make Do with Less

In the "make do with less" column would be somewhat obvious-sounding things like picking a smaller apartment, finding roommates, or moving to a cheaper neighborhood. Less obvious strategies might include finding an apartment with multiple rooms, signing a lease by yourself, and

---

[13] OECD: "Housing Costs Over Income."

then leasing out the other rooms at higher monthly rents (thereby reducing your all-in effective rent costs).

Renters should be sure to look at the "fully-loaded" rent level, meaning that if brokers' fees and other up-front costs are associated with renting the apartment, these should be averaged out over the length of the lease, to derive the true cost per month. Likewise, if rent-free periods are included, those should be averaged out over the life of the lease.

Utilities such as water, electric, gas, and other monthly expenses factor into shelter costs, as well. Always keep an eye out for opportunities to switch providers to benefit from better service or lower costs. Similarly, reducing electricity usage by converting to LEDs, turning off the lights in rooms that are currently vacant, and unplugging appliances when they aren't in use could add up to meaningful savings in the electricity department over time.

Get the Same for Cheaper

Getting the same for cheaper would encompass any crafty techniques that would allow one to keep their same level of housing standard of living but for a less expensive price tag. Negotiating with the landlord to sign a longer lease in exchange for a cheaper monthly rent is one example of this. Shopping for apartments at off-peak times (peak is typically centered around the summer, with more competition from students and recent graduates) is another example. One could also search for newly developed buildings that may be running special promotions as they try to lease-up (typically, landlords are willing to cut a deal with the initial group of tenants). Finally, asking a landlord if they need any help around the property in exchange for cheaper rent could be a low-effort way to cut rental expenses (hey, worth a shot right?).

Whichever goal we are trying to achieve, our view is that it makes sense to focus the most amount of time on living expenses, as these typically far outweigh other cost categories.

Food Costs

Food costs are another large expense category. Food costs can be further broken up into (i) everyday, necessary ("nondiscretionary") food costs and (ii) eating out or going to restaurants ("discretionary" food and beverage expenses). With regard to necessary food costs, strategies to save more might include cooking or bringing homemade lunch to work versus eating takeout, going vegetarian for a few days a week, or buying dry goods/nonperishables in bulk. Bringing lunch from home can make a huge difference over time, because of the frequency of meals. Saving just $5 per meal on lunch throughout the year would yield $1,300 in additional cash and likely wouldn't involve sacrificing any of the numerous intangible benefits of going to a restaurant (i.e., social interactions and new experiences).[14] As seen in Phase 3, a lot could be done with that money. Simply repeating this savings every year and earning a 5% annual return would result in >$16,000 of wealth accumulated by the end of 10 years. A 10% annual return would clock in at roughly $20,000 by the end of the same 10-year period. Big numbers.

At the grocery store, shopping by unit price instead of total price can be a handy way to reduce expenses (typically most effective for nonperishable items or goods that can be stored). On the other hand, maintaining a healthy diet is key to long-term health and performance in the workplace (critical to long-term revenue-enhancing strategies), so don't forsake nutrition just to save on food costs.

---

[14] Assuming 5 working days per week and 52 weeks in the year.

On the discretionary food and beverage side ... eat out less. Eating out every now and then is totally fine, but if restaurants are consuming a large or increasing percentage of your income, give yourself a budget of X restaurants per month and try to stick to it. Sitting down adds about 15%–20% to a food bill versus getting takeout, because you have to factor in the tip. Also, take a moment to look over the menu before choosing a place to go with friends (no one wants to get caught at an expensive restaurant by accident).

Finally, we can consider bars and alcohol as a subset of food costs. Replacing a bar night with a house party is a direct way to cut costs (depending on how rambunctious you and your friends are), and overall, trying to shift the percentage of drinks consumed away from the bar (and reducing the number of drinks in general) should benefit the bottom line.

Transportation

Transportation costs are typically going to be comprised of (i) everyday commuting and transportation needs, and (ii) long-distance, one-off trips.

Everyday transportation needs could involve buying or leasing a car or taking some form of public transportation (subway, bus, flying drone?).

The decision whether to lease or buy a car is important. To the extent that low-cost financing is available, buying is usually going to be the best option over the long term. The reason behind this is relatively simple (we discuss a similar economic logic in the homeownership section): Most car loans can be paid off within five years, but the useful life of a car (if properly taken care of) is most likely well in excess of five years (maybe closer to 15), which means that after the loan is paid off, you get the use of the car for "free" (outside of fuel, maintenance/repair, and insurance). Leasing means that you will never own the car outright. The leasing company owns the car and by definition, they will be looking to turn a profit on the lease (this should trigger some alarm bells in your head—where do you think their profit is coming from? Hint: you).

Consider the following simplified example of a $20,000 car that can either be leased at $140/month or purchased with a five-year car loan at 5% interest. Assume that the car is taken care of reasonably well and therefore can be expected to last for 15 years. By the end of the 15-year time frame, the person who leases this car will have paid $25,200 = 15years*12months*$140/month (assuming that lease costs don't increase over that 15-year time frame, which is a big "if"). Meanwhile, the owner will have paid principal and interest totaling about $22,620 by the end of the five-year loan term and would owe nothing subsequent to that outside of repair and maintenance (putting gasoline or EV charging costs aside as they would apply in both cases). That's quite a difference (roughly $2,500, which is 13% of the original sticker price), and remember these are after-tax dollars, which could be put to use in some kick-ass investing strategies, instead of being spent on a car lease.

And this is just one (fairly inexpensive) car. Many families utilize multiple cars at the same time and may go through three or four car "cycles" during their lifetime. That's at least six to eight cars in total, and if we apply that same basic $2,500 savings estimate per car, then the total loss in savings would be $15,000 to $20,000, which doesn't even factor in the money that could be earned on that savings, properly invested.

Total 15-Year Lease Cost			Total 15-Year Ownership		
Years		15	Loan		$20,000
Months/Year		12	Years		5
Total Months		180	Total Months		60
Cost per Month	$	140	Interest Rate		5%
Total Cost	$	25,200	Estimated Monthly Payment	$	377
			Total Cost	$	22,620
			Total Interest Paid	$	2,620
Total Cost - Lease	$	25,200	Total Principal Paid		$20,000
Total Cost - Ownership	$	22,620			
Difference	$	2,580			

Figure 3.7: Lease versus own economics for cars.

There are certainly reasons to lease a car, such as having a shorter time period when a car is needed and preferring the flexibility (if one is expected to move to a big city or to another country soon for example). However, be careful of leasing if it is just to receive a new car every few years (unless of course you are working on a new formula for synthetic old-car smelling perfume and need to test out some different combinations).

With car ownership, there are likely opportunities to learn a bit on your own to lower repair and maintenance costs over time and extend the useful life of your vehicle. Learning how to replace a tire, change the oil, and perform other basic maintenance functions could end up saving you a lot of money. This concept of reducing costs by learning how to "earn the profits" of service providers is applicable to other aspects of cost cutting, as well (certainly on the home-ownership front and also in regard to learning to cook). This shouldn't come as a surprise, as one of the main conclusions of this book is that sticking to an education-first and learning mindset over long periods of time can produce very positive, tangible benefits for the bank account.

One final thing to note about buying versus leasing a car is that stretching expense-wise for a high-priced car is bound to hurt the personal finance picture quite a bit under both circumstances, but it might disproportionately affect the buyer of the car, because they are on the hook for all of the car loan payments, while the lessor might be able to get out of his or her contract before too much damage is done. As it is throughout Phase 2, the lesson here is to really scrutinize purchases and to really, really scrutinize large purchases, such as a car.

The opportunity to buy a used car shouldn't be overlooked when it comes to cutting transportation expenses. In 2021, for example, there were around 15 million new cars sold in the U.S., however the number of used cars sold was closer to 40 million.[15] The used market is large and filled with opportunities for the entrepreneurial buyer. Many cars that have recently gone off lease or are lightly used and a few years old are available at double-digit discounts to prices for new cars.

Other ways to save on transportation costs might be to carpool to work, or more creatively, even to find a friend who needs to borrow a car occasionally and "lease" your car to them when you aren't using it.

On the public transportation side, see if your employer offers a commuter benefits program, which would allow you to pay for your monthly expenses with pretax dollars. In general, paying for things with pretax dollars is a good idea, because it lowers your overall tax bill, thereby saving you money directly. To see this in action, consider paying $100 for a commuter benefits card. By paying for that card in a tax-deductible way, you lower your taxable income by $100. At a 35% tax rate, this is equivalent to saving $35 ($100 * 0.35) and reducing the after-tax cost of the commuter benefits card to $65.

Finally, with regard to one-off transportation costs such as buying a plane ticket or train ticket, try to book in advance to save on costs, or join

---

[15] Per data from Cox Automotive.

a frequent flyer program and try to ride with that airline more often, to receive benefits over time.

Toolkit Summary—Expense Optimization Checklist

- Understand major spending categories (reference your personal income statement).
- Develop useful budgets: The Current Budget shows annualized expenses based on what you spent last month. The Average Annual Budget shows annualized expenses based on what you spent in the past year. The Target Budget represents where you would like to be in terms of spending levels. Try the income-first or expense-first approach to generate the target budget. Fiddle with it. See what works.
- Iterate to drive down expenses.
- Focus on the largest categories first (a 5% reduction in housing costs is likely more significant than a 5% reduction in the TV streaming budget). Housing, food, and transportation deserve focus.

Savings and Long-term Goals

Making use of some of the strategies outlined earlier, and maintaining a thrifty mindset toward expenses, should propel our personal finance ship toward its target budget, which, combined with revenue enhancing strategies, can be expected to get our average savings levels on track. As mentioned previously, savings is the oxygen or fuel in our long-term wealth creation machine. It is the most crucial building block of financial independence. More savings means more ammo to invest in diverse opportunities, as we explore later, in Phase 3. The last item to cover here in Phase 2 is the concept of saving for specific goals, such as a home purchase, wedding, entrepreneurial opportunity, child education costs, or retirement.

The first step in goal-specific saving is to estimate the total cost and timing of the expense. This number represents the total amount of money that we will need to come up with at some future date to satisfy the particular expense. Since we don't have to come up with that money today—rather, it's a future expense—we don't have to put 100% of the expense aside all at once. Instead, smart capital allocators can use investing to meet their long-term goal-oriented savings by investing some amount of savings today and letting it grow to an adequate level in the future.

Hence, in addition to the estimated expense item, the second piece of information we need is an estimate of the annual returns we expect to earn on our investments.[16]

Once we have an estimate of (i) the total expense we will have to come up with at some point in the future, as well as (ii) an estimate of the annual percentage returns we can expect to achieve by investing our capital, we can work backward to solve for the total amount of savings we would need to put aside today in order to reach that goal.

Figure 3.8: Flow chart of how savings today meet large expenses in the future.

The formula that we'll use to calculate this is:

---

[16] Readers with a financial background will realize that we are describing a present value calculation here. For those who haven't learned about the mechanics of present value yet, just follow along as best as you can, as we discuss present value in greater detail in Phase 3, when we discuss investments.

Savings needed today = (expense in the future) / (1 + [percentage Return on Investment (ROI)])^(time until expense)

An example will help illustrate. Consider saving for a child's college expenses. We can estimate the total cost for these expenses by assuming that we will have to pay for four years of college, 15 to 20 years from now. If average college costs today are $35,000/year, then we can estimate what they will be in the future by compounding the price today by an inflation estimate. Higher education costs have been going up rapidly, so we will use a relatively high 3% cost inflation estimate and a 15-year time frame. 15 years from now, then, the $35,000/year cost will be 35,000*(1.03^15), or $54,000. The total four-year cost estimate would then be 4*$54,000 = $216,000. Quite a hefty sum!

With that total cost in mind, what would we have to save today to reach that goal? In other words, how much money do we have to invest today in order to end up with $216,000 15 years from now? The answer depends on our ability to generate investment returns. For example, say that with a reasonable degree of certainty we feel that we could generate a 6% annualized investment return on our capital over the 15-year period, which is somewhere between the long-term historical return on stocks and bonds. Breaking out the formula from above, we have: Savings today = $216,000/(1.06)^15, which simplifies to about $90,000. So, we would need to set aside $90,000 today to deal with this expense later on. The potential for scholarships and the ability to take out student loans might help bridge the gap down the line, but this example still illustrates the mechanics of saving for a long-term goal like higher education.

Note that if we are able to earn a 10% annualized return instead of the 6% we estimated, then we would only need to save $52,000 ($216,000 / (1+.10)^15). In that way, the ability to generate higher investment returns is clearly beneficial to our ability to meet long-term funding targets, because it reduces the total amount of savings we have to put aside today (freeing that money up for other investments or whatever use we can think of). One final note of caution in these calculations is that it typically makes sense to assume a conservative number for the percentage investment return. Choosing a smaller number gives us a higher probability of meeting or exceeding that return target, and therefore a better chance of being able to adequately fund our expense item.

A Special Note on Investment Income

As discussed in Phase 3, a strong personal investment program should lead to healthy returns on invested capital over time. That is, by the end of this book we should have a good framework in place to distribute a person's nest egg into the most efficient investment buckets. We can think of this as sending our money to work every day (a moderately well-dressed pile of cash reading the morning news on the subway next to us).

The annual income earned by our personal invested capital is ours to keep. This "investment income" isn't factored into our discussion of Phase 2, because here, we are focusing on ways to boost savings from everyday jobs and expenditures; but that doesn't make investment income any less real. However, we'll wait to discuss investment income (and returns more generally) until after we have learned how to generate the necessary savings.

To recap: In Phase 2, we take a closer look at the dynamics behind growing one's savings and some strategies for doing so, focusing on both the "top line" in terms of increasing revenue potential over the long term and the budgeting process for expenses and how a thrifty mindset and more strategic spending could increase cash flow.

Some of the high-level strategies to keep in mind are:

- Extending useful lives (especially on large capital goods such as a home, car, computer or other large electronics, etc.) by learning and "earning the profit" margin of some service providers;

- Buying used goods instead of new when available and of sufficient quality;

- Questioning large purchases (anything >$100 should get a look);

- Reducing unnecessary consumption (house parties instead of bar nights);

- Increasing the utilization of existing assets (such as renting out idle assets like spare rooms in a house, or letting someone drive your car for a fee when you aren't using it); and

- Delaying large purchases (putting that new car off for another year; a concept similar to extending useful lives).

Each of these strategies counts as part of having a prudent mindset and being analytical in your approach to saving. Over time, repetition should make these strategies easier to implement (i.e., the sixth oil change is probably going to be easier and quicker than the first). That's enhanced productivity, the key driver of long-term income growth.

Saving is only one piece of the puzzle in terms of long-term wealth creation, however. As we see in Phase 3, the real juice comes by plugging that savings into a strong investment program and then letting the joys of long-term compounding take over. Juice also comes from a variety of fruits, such as apples and oranges, but we shall hold that discussion for another time (unless there's an attractive orange tree investment that comes up, of course). Onwards.

Phase 3

Invest the Surplus

If you want to become really wealthy, you must have your money work for you.

Sir John Templeton, *Templeton Plan*

hase 3 is the exciting culmination of the groundwork laid thus far. Let's go team!! Following Phase 1: Know the Numbers and the Phase 2: Supercharge Savings, our capital is ready to go to work. It is our job to employ that capital through smart capital allocation decisions.

Capital allocation is the process of distributing savings into different investment buckets. Doing so efficiently will maximize the return on that savings and grow net worth, which is our primary goal. Capital allocation can take many forms, but those who do it well create a system that charts a path for their savings. Savings flows through this system over time, depositing cash into different investment buckets along the way. In Phase 3 we are going to build this system. Hard hats required.

At the core of our system sit the Three Heroes of Capital Allocation: Working Capital, Flex Capital, and Pure Investment Capital. These are the investment buckets into which savings flow. If there is one concept that I want my reader to absorb from this book, it is how to build and utilize the Three Heroes.

As we'll see, the first two Heroes are a bit more defensive in nature. Outside of a certain portion of Flex Capital, they typically provide a savings buffer that ensures we can go about our daily lives without needing to worry about being able to pay expenses. In contrast, the third Hero, Pure Investment Capital, is where we go on the offensive, taking calculated risks that will result in long-term payoffs in the form of a higher standard of living. This is where we invest and really make our money grow. Because of its importance, this chapter spends most of its time on Pure Investment Capital. During the Pure Investment Capital section, we pour the concrete for several foundational concepts in investing: diversification, optimization, and rebalancing.

The journey doesn't end with our third Hero, however. Afterwards, we take a big step into the dynamic world of active management, seen through the lens of security analysis, which is the evaluation of specific investment options. Active management is mostly relevant to Pure Investment Capital, but I present it separately because it is a longer discussion. As we'll see, active management is the rocket fuel of the capital allocation process. Again, hard hats —and maybe space suits—required.

Working through the basics of active management, we develop tools to identify, analyze, and execute on new investments. If history is any guide, there will be plenty of attractive opportunities to evaluate over one's financial lifetime.

By the end of Phase 3, our capital will have been shipped off to work, and we'll be reaping the benefits.

One thing to note is that in Phase 3 we are really discussing what to do with our financial assets such as cash, stocks, bonds, investment funds, etc. Physical or non-financial assets such as a house or car are important but aren't the focus here. Housing in particular has many investment characteristics but is discussed in greater detail during Part 2 of this book.

The Three Heroes of Capital Allocation

By this point in the book, we have mapped out our financial profile and optimized our savings accumulation. These efforts have built the savings engine, which means that the simple passage of time should lead to material growth in the nest egg. Cold hard cash, looking for a job and eager to get started.

Once we've saved up this capital, where should we put it so that our money is gainfully employed and working hard? The sock drawer? Under the mattress? Neither of these is likely to lead to long-term capital appreciation or financial independence. Plus, where would we put our socks? Flip flops can only get you so far after all and I still can't figure out if Crocs are stylish or not.

Effective capital allocation could mean the difference between increasing our wealth at, say, a 3% annual rate, or something higher like an 8% annual rate. These efforts pay off big time. For example, over 30 years, that 8% rate would produce wealth that is more than four times that of the 3% rate.

Having a framework in place is important because we don't have to think as hard about these decisions in real time. The process of putting dollars in different places becomes automatic, which frees up time to examine interesting individual investing options or to figure out more efficient places to put our socks.

What I refer to as the Three Heroes of Capital Allocation represents my view of an effective model for putting one's savings to work. The Three Heroes are:

1. Working Capital

2. Flex Capital

3. Pure Investment Capital

Each Hero has its own specific purpose in one's financial framework, as well as its own snazzy spandex-heavy wardrobe. We can think of savings that is coming in as cascading through these three Heroes one after the other, depositing some capital in each along the way. This "waterfall" framework explains the order of the Three Heroes; they progress, from one to the next, and that is how they are presented here, starting with Working Capital.

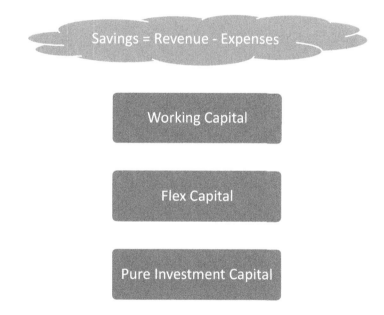

Figure 4.1: Waterfall of savings into buckets representing the Three Heroes of Capital Allocation.

Working Capital

Working Capital represents the dollars utilized to satisfy one's day-to-day spending. It is an active pile of money that is constantly being drained by expenses and refilled by earnings. For most people, the Working Capital account is their checking account, functioning like a well-loved coffee mug. It doesn't hold much, it is used a few times a day (more if the previous night included much partying and little sleep), but it is dependable and you can't live without it.

Cash that sits in the Working Capital account is likely to earn very little in the way of interest (at the time of writing, the national average for interest paid on checking accounts was 0.04%[17]—not exactly tantalizing) so the more efficiently one can run this account—while still being conservative so as to avoid a cash shortfall—the better for long-term investment results. In other words, building up excess amounts in the Working Capital account can negatively impact long-term wealth creation, because the cash is sitting there, idle. Excess capital in the working capital account is like sending your money to work only to find out that it is napping on the job half the day. As soon as we hit a satisfactory amount in the Working Capital account, the extra dollars should be airlifted out to the next two Heroes.

My view is that a reasonable amount of cash to keep in the Working Capital account is two to three months' worth of expenses to be able to cover larger on-time costs that pop up from time to time—such as a deposit on an apartment rental or plane tickets for a vacation. Having the extra padding in the Working Capital account means we can satisfy these costs without having to take money out of our other accounts or borrow. So, if we envision a person starting from scratch with no savings and

---

[17] Source: FDIC: "National Rates and Rate Caps."

$2,000 a month in expenses, the Working Capital account could be built up to about $4,000 to $6,000. It might make sense to look at the last 12 months of spending and take something closer to the max-spending month as your baseline vs. the average, just to be on the safe side.

The Working Capital account is the first stop for money coming in and out on a regular basis because income is direct deposited into it and expenses are paid out of it (either with a debit card or by linking this account to a credit card). So, even though the proportion of savings allocated to this account may be relatively small, it should be set up and monitored carefully.

This means choosing a reputable bank with strong marks for service and access to an ATM network—or a reduction in ATM fees for using an out-of-network ATM. There are multiple websites that can help you research and choose a primary bank to work with for everyday checking account needs. For example, Nerdwallet is a great resource in terms of researching specific checking accounts. This checking account should be FDIC insured, to protect deposits up to a certain amount (currently $250,000). Some newer financial products that are similar to checking accounts—such as Venmo or the Square Cash app—may not be FDIC insured.

The cryptocurrency industry serves as a cautionary tale about the importance of FDIC insurance. At the time of writing, several cryptocurrency companies have recently failed that had offered their customers something that looked a lot like a savings account but instead held cryptocurrency and wasn't FDIC insured. Users could deposit their crypto and be paid interest at highly attractive rates. For the most part, users ignored the fact that these accounts weren't FDIC-insured. When these crypto-banks failed due to declines in prices of the crypto-universe, the users were left unable to withdraw their capital and may ultimately be forced to suffer large losses. This would have been a nonfactor had the users kept their capital in accounts with FDIC insurance.

Flex Capital

After the Working Capital account is sufficiently funded, we can move to the second Hero of Capital Allocation: Flex Capital.

The Flex Capital account is a longer-term but still liquid account that serves two purposes. Its first big job is to protect against adverse developments or unforeseen expenses—such as a sudden job loss or major medical bill—that would otherwise drain the Working Capital account. It serves as a place to store emergency funds. Its second job is to hold opportunistic cash, so we can take advantage of interesting investments that surface. This could include a stock market downturn or a recession—in which investment bargains typically abound—or a private business opportunity such as one taking advantage of your view that with genetic modifications, oranges could be even MORE orange. This second opportunistic function is akin to building up a war chest that can be used to pounce on attractive investments.

In this way, the second Hero of Capital Allocation serves the twin, flexible purposes of defense, by protecting against drawdowns in Working Capital, and offense, by standing ready to bring in the cavalry if attractive investments are found. To serve this dual mandate, it is important that the dollars held in this pool are easily accessible and liquid—which means they can be converted to cash without much hassle. Because large drawdowns in Working Capital, or rare investment opportunities, only come along so often, we can tie up the capital in this pool for a little bit longer (i.e., sacrifice liquidity a little more) than we would in the Working Capital account.

Flex Capital account	
Emergency Funds: Reserves to protect against unexpected drawdowns in the Working Capital account	**Opportunistic Funds**: War Chest to take advantage of attractive investment opportunities

Figure 4.2: Illustration of components in the Flex Capital account.

Most of the time, the best place for this Flex Capital money is in a savings account. I suggest a high-yield savings account, although given its partial function as a war chest, gold doubloons stored in one's moated castle may suffice. High-yield savings accounts pay a little more in interest (~2.15% at the time of writing) than a regular checking account does, but still offer assurance of principal and usually at least 7- to 10-day liquidity— meaning that cash can be withdrawn upon 7 to 10 days' notice. Importantly, high-yield savings accounts are also likely to be FDIC-insured, meaning that we aren't risking any of our principal by stashing extra dollars there.

A possible subset of the Flex Capital account is the certificate of deposit (CD). These are financial products offered by banks that allow investors to earn a slightly higher rate of return on their cash, in exchange for locking up their funds for a longer period of time. Whereas the typical high-yield savings account might let you withdraw funds in 7 to 10 days, a CD might be offered for anywhere from three months to a year or more, in exchange for a higher interest rate. Hence, investors should be careful not to stash too much of their Flex Capital in CDs, due to the unpredictability of when they might need access to these funds. One strategy would be to take just a portion of the Flex Capital, amounting to at most 20% to 50% of the account, and invest it in a CD. Money market funds may be an alternative place relative to CDs to store Flex Capital to earn a bit of extra yield.

At the time of writing, Goldman Sachs, SoFi, Ally Bank, and others offer high-yield savings accounts that are easy to set up and provide competitive interest rates. As always, you should do some background research on financial providers, to see which one suits you best.

The amount of money to invest in the Flex Capital account can vary dramatically, but because of its dual purpose of defense (emergency funds) and offense (war chest), a good rule of thumb might be to build this account up to one to two times the balance in the Working Capital account (between two months of expenses on the low end and six months on the high end). The emergency fund portion of the account should stay relatively stable (not to be touched outside of actual emergencies) while the war chest portion can vary a bit more.

As mentioned above, once the Working Capital account has been sufficiently funded, any excess cash should be airlifted out. The first stop for this airlifted cash should likely be the Flex account, until it, too, reaches a satisfactory level. Unlike the Working Capital account, however, we shouldn't fret too much if excess funds accumulate in the Flex account over and above the one to two times Working Capital rule of thumb level. That's because excess funds sit in our war chest and can stay there earning some level of interest until some outsized investment opportunities surface.

That means, be patient with the war chest portion of Flex Capital until there are exceptional opportunities. As always, a quote from Buffett will help add color to this point:

The trick in investing is just to sit there and watch pitch after pitch go by and wait for the one right in your sweet spot. And if people are yelling, "Swing, you bum!" ignore them.

Warren Buffett, on baseball and investing

The right size of the war chest portion of the Flex Capital account depends on a combination of (i) investor risk preferences and (ii) the backdrop for investment returns at the moment. I like to think of the war chest as money that should be invested when markets have sold off quite a bit; the more markets sell off, the more money should be invested, to earn attractive long-term returns. Viewing market sell-offs in a historical context can be helpful here. For example, peak to trough (top to bottom) declines in the stock market, as proxied by the S&P 500® index, were about 50% in the 2008 financial crisis, 45% in the dot-com bust, and 30% in the 1987 Black Monday stock market crash (three large-scale financial meltdowns that took place within the past 50 years). In addition, the S&P 500 declined more than 30% from its prior peak in the Covid-19 panic sell-off in March 2020, according to Yahoo Finance.

Investors have a tendency to panic as markets decline and grow increasingly fearful the longer the selloff lasts; no one likes watching the value of their investment account fall. However, when viewed in the context of the war chest, as markets go from down 10% to down 20%, we should be gaining confidence that we are getting closer to the "bottom," which means that the chances of earning attractive returns on war chest capital are growing. Buy low, sell high.

When markets appear to have been on a tear and prices are high, it could make sense to allocate proportionally more of one's savings to the Flex account for safe keeping, and replenish the war chest, rather than investing directly in the market during these frothier periods. Likewise, when markets are in free fall and others are panicking, it could be time to drain the war chest and make some great long-term investments. As Buffett famously put it, the objective is to "be fearful when others are greedy, and greedy when others are fearful."

This is not to say that falling markets are inherently a good thing or that investing when something is going down is a surefire way to make money on a rebound. Rather, all else being equal, the cheaper one can buy an asset they like, the better. As always, it pays to do some homework and be patient. Sometimes the clearance sale at Best Buy offers can't-miss deals on flatscreen TVs, but sometimes, those are last year's plasmas and aren't worth the trouble, despite the markdown. Regardless, without banking some capital in the Flex account, we wouldn't have the ability to participate in these moments.

An example might help illustrate the Flex account in action. Let's say Maria has a Working Capital account of $3,000. A proper amount to keep in the Flex account would be one to two times that—so $3,000 to $6,000. By Maria's analysis of her financial situation and expenses, she feels comfortable that $2,000 is the right amount for her to keep in the Flex account in case of an emergency. Thus, the remaining $1,000 to $4,000 is her war chest. As her expenses grow over time, maybe the amount she wants to reserve for emergencies grows beyond the initial $2,000. Likewise, if she isn't finding attractive investment opportunities, she might let the war chest portion of the Flex account grow (perhaps her overall balance increases to $10,000 while she waits to invest). The choice—and flexibility—are hers to command.

The important thing to keep in mind with Flex Capital is that the flexibility should work for you – not the other way around. For example, if you are struggling to get invested, you shouldn't feel like you must wait until you have maximized your Flex Capital before starting to put money into Pure Investment Capital. Once the account is established with a bit of cash in it, the active management of it is up to you and your specific saving and investing goals. For someone with $2,000 in expenses, the guidelines presented above would result in at least $4,000 set aside in

Working Capital and another $4,000 in Flex Capital – a total of $8,000 to be set aside before moving on to Pure Investment Capital. This might be too high a bar for some, or too low a threshold for others, so feel free to play around with whichever account configurations give you the greatest comfort and security while still allowing you to hit those long-term financial goals.

Pure Investment Capital

After splashing in the shallow waters of Working Capital, and then swimming downstream to make a deposit in the Flex account, our savings have made it to the ocean: Pure Investment Capital. Getting to this point means that we have taken care of funding our everyday expenses and stashed extra money on the side, for unforeseen life events. It also means that we've held some cash in reserve, in case we find some really good investment opportunities. After doing so, we feel confident that our basic needs are taken care of, and we now have the opportunity to grow our wealth by investing in areas with higher expected returns.

As I've alluded to throughout this book, the wonderful thing about saving and investing is that, when done well, our money can go to work for us all day, at night, and on weekends, without our having to expend extra effort outside of analyzing our capital allocation options. Our money never gets tired. Snowstorms, heat waves, and car trouble be darned, capital still clocks in every day. This is passive wealth creation and one likely reason that Einstein reportedly called the compounding effect of investment dollars the eighth wonder of the world.

Creating a well-diversified portfolio with a solid expected return is within the reach of all of us with savings, and, generally, the more ya' know, the more ya' money grows (or something like that).

Most of the action in terms of our passive wealth creation comes as the result of decisions we make with our Pure Investment Capital. This stuff can really move the needle. After all, money in the Working Capital and Flex Capital accounts is likely to earn only minimal interest. Outside of the war chest, money sits in those funds for purposes other than long-term wealth creation (such as funding our everyday cash expenses and saving for a rainy day). Once those bases are covered, though, we are free to redirect excess dollars into the best long-term investments we can find, and there are multiple strategies for doing so.

Importantly, the Pure Investment Capital portion of our journey is where readers get to exercise their creative muscles and study, explore, and evaluate exciting new businesses and market opportunities. As we shall see, in many ways, the actively minded investor gets to play the role of detective, scientist, strategist, poker player, and other fascinating vocations all at once, and at their leisure. Few other pursuits offer this level of multifaceted intellectual stimulation.

For the discission of Pure Investment Capital, we will introduce the Third Master Formula, alongside basic investment concepts such as returns, risk, and inflation. Then, we break the investible universe up into distinct asset classes and dive into the foundational pillars of capital allocation: diversification, optimizing risk/return, and rebalancing over time. Let's get the ball rolling.

The Third Master Formula

For our foray into Pure Investment Capital, we need Our Third Master Formula, which describes how investors profit. It shows that our investments are a function of how much money we start out with (principal) multiplied by a factor representing the returns on that money.

The formula is:

Investments = Principal*Returns

Returns are another word for profit, and when expressed as a percentage, they represent the rate at which our money today grows into money in the future. The returns part of the formula is, as we will see, itself comprised of the annualized return on the positions we take, as well as the time during which those returns are compounded.

For simplicity, risk isn't expressly identified in the formula, but it plays a key role in our investing framework.

Investors will be hard pressed to embark on their journey to financial freedom without encountering veritable monsoons of information about risk and return. What do people mean when they mention these terms, why do they come up so often, and why should we care? In addition, investors even edge out basketball pump salesmen in the amount of time they spend discussing inflation. Is inflation really that big a deal? How does it work? Over the next few pages, we will introduce each of these concepts, because they underpin our strategies and decision-making frameworks for the remainder of Phase 3.

Return From Where?

In an investment context, the word "return" simply refers to the profits we earn on investments. When we make an investment, we give someone our capital, and in return we expect to be repaid, with a profit. Positive returns mean that we are making money (we were returned more than we gave), while negative returns mean that we are losing money (we were returned less than we gave). Typically, we measure investment returns as a percentage representing the profits earned as a proportion of the initial investment. Over multiple periods, we can even earn returns on our returns (profits on our profits), which is a concept called compounding returns. More on that below.

As investors, one primary goal is to maximize percentage returns, and to do that we need to understand the mechanics of how money grows. In the introduction to this book, I launched the discussion of compound interest using a story about a queen, a traveling sage, and some rice, and then got a bit more granular (rice pun intended) about what that looked like in mathematical form. Many investors describe compound interest as a snowball rolling from the top of a hill to the bottom. As it rolls down the hill, the snowball becomes bigger, faster, and more powerful. If it runs into a parent holding coffee, the kids are going to have to eat double vegetables tonight.

As a refresher, let's return to the formula for compound returns:[18]

Future Value = Principal*(1 + annual rate of return) ^ time in years

Future value, the output on the left, is what we get if we take the principal and invest it at a certain rate for a certain number of years.

Consider a person who makes a $100 investment that promises to pay 5% interest at the end of one year and also return the $100 of principal at that time. At the end of the year, then, our investor will receive the interest—$100*5% = $5—plus the original $100 principal. So, the investor's total account value will be $105. Put otherwise, using some basic algebra, the future value of $105 = $100*5% + $100, which can be rewritten as:

$105 = $100*(1+5%).[19]

---

[18] Readers will note the similarity between the compound return formula and the Third Master Formula. In fact, they describe the same process by which money today grows into money in the future.

[19] In this example, the time in years is 1.

This matches up with our compound return formula, above.

The concept of compounding comes into play here in Year 2, because now, the investor can earn interest on the $5 profit earned in Year 1. The snowball is gathering momentum. That is, in Year 2, the investment formula becomes $105*(1+5%) = $110.25. So, while in Year 1, we made $5 in interest, in Year 2, we made $5.25, which is 5% more without us adding any principal. Although this may not sound like much, as we'll see, compound interest can produce spectacular results over time. A couple snowflakes here and there can turn into a legendary igloo.

Growth of $100 Using Compound Interest		
Principal - Year 1 Beginning (A)	$	100.00
Interest Rate (B)		5%
Interest in Year 1 (A*B)	$	5.00
Account Value - Year 1 Ending	**$**	**105.00**
Principal - Year 2 Beginning	$	105.00
Interest Rate		5%
Interest in Year 2	$	5.25
Account Value - Year 2 Ending	**$**	**110.25**

Figure 4.3: Growth of principal according to compound interest.

Consider that same 5%-per-year investment over a 20-year time frame. Without the power of compound interest, we would have made $5/year for 20 years, or $100 in total profits. Combined with our initial $100 investment, this means that our account value at the end of Year 20 would be $200 ($100 of principal + $100 of profit). With compound interest, however, the account would be worth approximately $265 (=$100*(1.05^20)), an increase of more than 30% over the same account without compound interest. The gap gets even wider as time goes on (by

Year 30, we would have more than 70% more, because of compound interest. By Year 50, we would have more than 200% more).

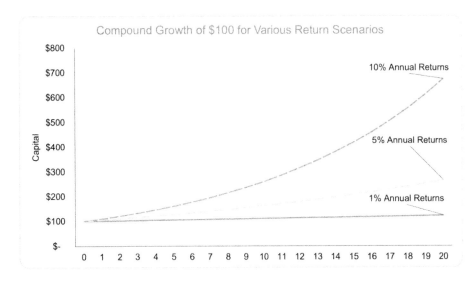

Figure 4.4: Graph of principal growth for various compound return scenarios.

There are a few key takeaways from this discussion of investment returns so far.

First, the more principal that one starts out with, the greater value the portfolio is likely to have in the future—which is why a robust savings program is really important. Savings is raw material in the search for wealth accumulation and financial freedom. More savings means more of that labor reserve going to work every day alongside us and, as we multiply the savings, we multiply the output of that workforce.

Second, higher rates of return can produce large differences in wealth over time. So, the same level of savings can produce very different outcomes, depending on the efficacy of the investment program. For example, it might not matter exactly how much you save if you put it into an ice cream store that is only open in the winter and whose primary flavor of ice cream is Frozen Shrimp.

A quick look at Figure 4.4 shows how much faster $100 grows when it is invested at 10%, rather than at just 1%. Working hard and saving gives us the chance to earn high returns on our money but doesn't guarantee those returns. That's why we spend time considering investment options, in Phase 3. Earning higher returns is akin to having more highly trained workers that are above-average producers for us.

Third, time plays a really important role in investment returns. The longer the time horizon, the exponentially larger a nest egg we could be left with (and the more massive the snowball). That's why starting early and sticking to a program are important and why working hard to make sure you are putting money aside to invest is generally the right move. Long time horizons also play a major role in reducing risk, as we'll see, because, all else being equal, a longer time horizon decreases the probability that one-time events, mistakes, or poor market conditions derail our results. So, even if someone isn't sure they're ready to start investing, they'll find that getting just a little bit going can make a big difference over time.

Risky Business

Although understanding returns is vitally important, just knowing the profit potential of an investment isn't enough, because there is always some probability that things won't turn out as we expect. That is risk. The concept of risk implies uncertainty about future outcomes. Risk means that if we were rolling a snowball down a hill and aimed it at a tree, then sometimes the snowball is going to hit a rock halfway down and lose one-tenth of its snow, or it might veer off to the side because of a gust of wind and miss the tree. A teenager on a snow tube might come crashing through and run into our kinetic ice missile. Anything can happen.

For example, let's say we have two options: (1) invest $100 and earn a $100 profit with 100% probability, or (2) invest $100 and earn a $100 profit with 50% probability, a $125 profit with 25% probability, and a $75 profit with 25% probability. In Option (2) we have an equal probability of making an extra $25 or losing an extra $25. Over time, we would expect to make and lose the extra $25 with the same frequency, so these options are expected to cancel each other out. That is, our expected value for Option 2 is $100 of profit on average. Given those choices, most people would take Option 1. Option 2 encompasses a lot more uncertainty about the future outcome of the investment, even though, based on the probabilities, we would expect each option to produce the same result of $200 over time. Investors would generally agree that Option 2 is a lot riskier—and unnecessarily so because we don't get paid to take that risk. Figure 4.5 provides a graphic depiction of these choices.

Figure 4.5: Expected value of an investment in two different risk scenarios.

Many investments, especially those in the stock market, bring with them plenty of uncertainty about future outcomes. When we buy a stock, we can take a view of how successful that business will be in the future and how its cash flow might grow. We can also take an educated guess about how those cash flows will be valued by investors in the market, and therefore, at what price we think the stock will trade. Guessing isn't knowing, though. There is always the possibility that things will turn out differently than we expect. With something as complex as analyzing stocks, the range of outcomes can be large.

In any investment context, there are multiple kinds of risk and uncertainty. Understanding what those risks are and how they interact with each other is the real challenge. One of the key lessons from legendary value investor Marty Whitman is that the word "risk" doesn't imply much without an adjective in front of it.

For example, there are market risks (the risk of whether prices will go up or down), there is investment risk (the probability that a company's profitability will decline or the enterprise becomes permanently impaired), there is liquidity risk (in regard to being able to buy or sell without impacting the price), regulatory risk, tax risk, and a whole host of other risks that can come in and out of focus.

The type of risk that we typically care most about is investment risk, or the potential for real business values to be impaired. Here's an example of investment risk: If I own a fruit cart and one day, I come to work and realize that a clever squirrel has made off with my fruit and set my cart on fire, then my business has just suffered a permanent impairment (assuming my cart isn't insured against squirrel attacks). In other words, my business value has just declined. Further, if my sister was the one who had invested the initial capital to get my fruit cart going, then she just suffered an investment loss (negative return) due to the decline in my business' value. Thanksgiving is going to be awkward this year.

Many financial market participants seem to focus primarily on market risk—that is, whether security prices will go up or down in the future. My view, which was heavily influenced by Marty Whitman, is that it is much more helpful to think about investment risk and real business values, and to try to buy assets at good prices, than it is to fret over shorter-term fluctuations in markets. Over the long term, if a business is successful and the investor doesn't significantly overpay for what they buy, things will tend to work out.

Savvy investors often use the market's wild gyrations as an opportunity to pick up bargains at discounts to what they believe intrinsic value—a concept of "true worth" that we will discuss—is or will be in the future. The real issue is not whether Apple will beat earnings by 5% or 10% this quarter, but whether Apple will still be relevant in 15 years. Will Apple's underlying earnings power be higher or lower than it is today? How confident are we? These are important questions about investment risk.

Combining Risk and Return to Make Profitable Investment Decisions

Risk and return are closely related concepts. Each investment is going to have some level of risk and some level of expected return. Whenever we put our money to work, we expect to earn a profit (return). But we usually won't have an assurance that our profit will materialize; there is some risk that it won't. Balancing these factors is a central task for investors, so we will take a look below at some ways to start to combine risk and return when investing.

Generally, risk and return move in tandem: to increase returns, investors take on more risk, in some form. Here's a real-world example. Consider the differences between a Treasury bond that is issued by the U.S. government compared to a corporate bond issued by a U.S. company, such as IBM. Generally, U.S. government bonds are considered to have a very remote probability of defaulting (i.e., not being able to meet interest and principal payments). The U.S. government has vast resources at its disposal, including a massive tax base and the ability to literally (albeit indirectly) print money. As a result, government bonds carry a very low interest rate, as they are seen as having the lowest risk of defaulting.

In comparison, a corporate bond issued by a U.S. company such as IBM is going to have a relatively higher probability of default. Unlike the U.S. government, IBM cannot print money or raise taxes to finance shortfalls in its profits. All else being equal, the IBM corporate bond carries more investment risk. As we would expect, then, the corporate bond is going to have a higher yield (or expected return) relative to the U.S. government bond. So, our more risk = more return concept holds, and in the broader market, this phenomenon is a critical force influencing investment outcomes. To illustrate, at the time of writing, the 10-year U.S. Treasury bond trades with a yield of ~4.0%, while the IBM bonds maturing roughly 10 years from now trade for yields in the 5.5% range (a full 1.5% higher).[20] Investors are receiving an extra 1.5% per year to take on the risk of investing in IBM bonds instead of government bonds.

For a more generalized depiction, Figure 4.6 shows the yield on a group of corporate bonds[21] compared to the yield on 10-year government bonds issued by the U.S. Treasury over time. The line represents the difference between returns on the corporate bonds relative to the Treasury bonds. Note that the difference is always positive, meaning that corporate bonds always have a higher yield than government bonds do, which corresponds to their relative levels of risk. Same concept as above, just in picture form.

---

[20] According to data from FINRA.
[21] Those rated Baa by Moody's.

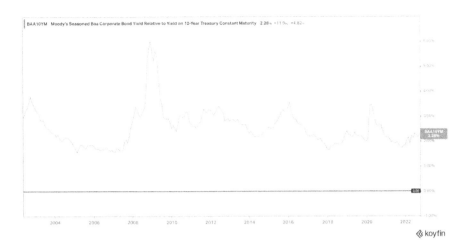

Figure 4.6: Bond yields versus 10-year Treasury yields.

Source: Koyfin (www.Koyfin.com), with reference to Moody's

Also note that over time, this "spread"—the difference between the rates—has varied from as low as 1% in frothier markets to as high as 6%, in times of crisis. The spread was close to 4% when the Covid-19 pandemic struck in March 2020, for example, meaning that corporate bonds were priced to yield almost 4% more than Treasury bonds were. Investors were very nervous that defaults on corporate bonds were going to rise. Changes in spread have to do with changes in the market's view of the relative riskiness of corporate versus government bonds. The higher the spread, the more risk is being baked into the corporate bonds. Investors sometimes refer to this as a "credit risk premium," because investors in the corporate bonds are taking on excess credit risk, given that the corporation may not pay them back.

For the same reason that a corporate bond generally offers a higher expected return than a Treasury bond does, so, too, an equity or share of stock in a company offers a higher expected return and higher level of investment risk than a corporate bond does. The risk and expected return on IBM stock should be more than the risk and return on IBM bonds, because bondholders are technically lending the company money, for which they get favorable treatment. (In this way, the bondholders act as "teacher's pet." No spitballs, please.)

As creditors, bondholders have a contractual right to be paid back first, before stockholders receive anything. It follows that a stock is going to carry a higher investment risk than a bond, and typically over time, stocks have delivered higher returns than bonds do. Morningstar estimates that since 1926, stocks have produced close to 10% annualized returns, compared to 5% to 6% returns for bonds.[22] So, again, higher investment risk tends to correspond to higher returns.

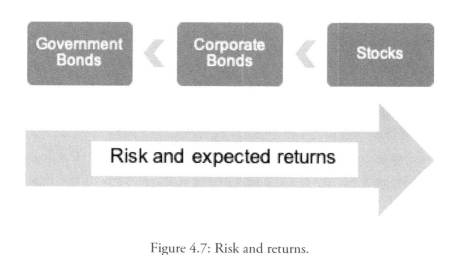

Figure 4.7: Risk and returns.

Don't worry if this example doesn't entirely click yet. I offer it to help explain how investors think about the relative attractiveness of different

---

[22] CNN Money: "How Do Bond Returns Compare with Stock Returns?"

investment options. Hopefully, by the end of this chapter, the concepts of risk versus return will become familiar and accessible to new investors.

This general framework of the way that risk and return tend to interact with each other is helpful as a foundation for understanding investing and is the reason we choose three distinct pools of capital—Working Capital, Flex Capital, and Pure Investment Capital—and present them according to their risk and return levels. Working Capital will be invested at the lowest risk and lowest expected return, while Investment Capital will generally carry higher average levels of risk and expected return.

Combining risk and return in investing is very similar to doing a cost-benefit analysis or a pros and cons list for any other decision. It isn't that different from deciding which movie to go see at the new 5-D cinema that just opened in town. The monster flick has Ben Affleck in it playing a zombie Sunglass Hut salesman, which could be cool, but the plot might stink, and then you've wasted two and a half hours and some of your hard-earned savings. You think you would enjoy the movie, but it might not work out. Is it worth it?

The best investment opportunities typically arise when we can get a lot of return while taking very little risk. Getting practice spotting these situations can really enhance one's portfolio. It would be like waiting until there was a 75% off coupon and a satisfaction guarantee for that monster movie. The risk is substantially lower than it was before, so it is a more attractive investment of time and money. Plus, who wouldn't want to see Zombie Ben Affleck try to hawk some Ray-Bans?

Inflation—But Not the Kind that Leads to Relaxing in a Floating Chair in Your Friend's Pool

Any introduction to investing would be incomplete without spending a little time on inflation. Those of us perusing the business news find frequent mentions of this all-important and dynamically mysterious concept. Simply put, inflation refers to the general rise in prices for goods and services over time. In 1930, a newspaper might have cost you 5 cents. Today, it's $1.50. Median home prices in 1950 were $7,400, while by 2010, they had reached $220,000.[23] These are both outcomes of a generally inflationary economy: one in which prices for similar items tend to go up, rather than down, over time.

Inflation is an important concept, because it represents a headwind against your purchasing power (i.e., how much "stuff" you can buy). To see why, consider a situation where you want to save up for a house. If you wanted to buy this house today, it might cost you $300,000. If you have saved up $300,000 and are ready to buy your new house, then this is no problem. But say that you have saved up $300,000 and you don't want to buy your house until 10 years from now. All else being equal, if home price inflation is 2% per year, then the house that costs $300,000 today will cost $365,700 by the time you are ready to buy it (=300,000*(1.02^10)). This means that you will either have to save up more money in the meantime (either by working or investing), or you will have to settle for a cheaper house, when you are finally ready to buy.

More generally, since the level of prices tends to go up a few percentage points per year, holding cash that earns a very low interest rate means that the amount one can buy (of goods/services or investment opportunities) with a certain amount of savings is going to decline every year. In the case

---

[23] *Curbed*: "Why Buying a House Today Is So Much Harder Than in 1950."

of inflation, standing still (not investing) is equivalent to moving backward (losing purchasing power). That's why I talk about the dangers of holding too much cash over long periods of time. Investors should aim to earn returns that at least match the level of inflation, to maintain their purchasing power. More purchasing power = good. Less purchasing power = bad.

In rare situations throughout history, inflation has really gotten out of control and led to the destabilization of societies. Those in need of a good scary story to tell on family camping trips should take a Wikipedia ride over to the page for German hyperinflation in the 1920s, to see how that nation began printing currency in response to reparations payments resulting from World War I.

As the government printed more and more marks (the German currency at the time), the value in purchasing power of each mark declined dramatically per unit of external currency, such as the U.S. dollar. Everyday goods, such as bread, skyrocketed in price because of the reduced purchasing power of the German currency. A loaf of bread that would have cost 160 marks in 1922 cost an astonishing 200,000,000,000 marks, just a year later. That's a lot of zeroes. Those who had saved and held their savings in German-denominated cash saw those savings devalued and essentially wiped out in a very short span of time. People carted around paper money in wheelbarrows to go to the grocery store and literally burned currency because they couldn't afford coal to heat their homes. This created enormous social and economic stress for the country and acted as a destabilizing force in the years ahead. Episodes of hyperinflation such as this are quite rare, but investors should still understand them to avoid repeating the mistakes of the past.

With a solid understanding of key investing concepts such as return, risk, and inflation, we can move on to applying these and other ideas to build an investment portfolio, starting with an outline of the different investment options that exist.

The Five Asset Classes

Let's take a look at different kinds of investments available to the average capital allocator. Broadly speaking, these are the different types of places in which to deploy savings to earn returns, and so, it is important to understand them. One might think of the investable asset classes that follow as distinct superpowers of the Hero of Pure Investment Capital, with each having its own risk and return attributes. For purposes of discussion, these asset classes are:

1. Cash

2. Federal and municipal government debt

3. Corporate fixed income (debt and preferred stock)

4. Equities (common stocks)

5. Private assets, derivatives, and other

Let's take them one by one.

Cash:

Within our Working Capital and Flex Capital Accounts, we should have already built up a sizable cash buffer, so any cash sitting within a Pure Investment Account should be relatively minimal. Cash in these accounts will typically represent deposited monies that haven't yet been invested: cash that has made it off the plane but hasn't checked into the hotel.

Investment income from bonds or dividend income from stock holdings might also cause a buildup of cash in the investment account.

Remember that cash earns very little in terms of interest, and so large cash holdings in the Pure Investment Account should typically be avoided. That said, there is some favorable optionality to holding a chunk of cash in the Investment Account, to be able to act on opportunities quickly, given that it could take a week or longer to access funds from the war chest in the Flex Account. Professional investors call this "dry powder," in that it stands ready to make some explosive returns when opportunities arise.

Federal and Municipal Government Debt:

As noted earlier, federal government debt (for example, Treasury bonds) is typically thought of as the lowest-risk security that one can find. "T-Bills," which are treasury bonds with a maturity (time to expiration) of less than a year, can be a good alternative to holding cash, as the investment principal is all but assured, and the interest rate on T-bills is typically at least a little bit higher than that on idle cash.

State and local governments can also issue bonds, which are typically referred to as "municipal bonds," or "munis," for short. Often, these bonds are issued to fund certain infrastructure projects such as bridges, toll roads, schools, or public trampoline parks, but they may also be what are known as general obligation bonds, with no explicit purpose. State and local governments don't have the ability to run persistent fiscal deficits (i.e., spending more than they take in in tax revenue), can't print money as the federal government can, and may have less diversified economic drivers—for example, a town dominated by a large manufacturing plant. To account for this increased risk, the yield on municipal bonds is usually higher than that available on Treasuries that are issued by the federal government.

An interesting quirk about federal and municipal debt is that there may be favorable tax treatment of the interest income earned on these investments. The income from treasury bonds, for example, is exempt from state and local taxes, while, depending on the specific bond and where the investor resides, the income from municipal bonds may not be taxed at all.

Corporate Fixed Income:

Similarly to how governments issue debt, corporations are constantly raising money by issuing bonds or other fixed-income securities, such as preferred stock. Fixed income just means that an investor receives periodic payments that have been set by the company raising money; the income is fixed. Corporate bonds typically carry a higher interest rate than federal and municipal debt does, because of the higher historical default rates for corporations We discussed this in the section on risk and returns, above. IBM can't go to the printing press to create money to pay its debts, and raising prices may not be easy for IBM, compared to the government's ability to hike tax rates. In general, the higher interest rates on corporate bonds compensate investors for this greater riskiness.

Ratings companies such as S&P and Moody's publish their opinions on the safety of corporate bonds. These opinions reflect how risky the ratings agency thinks that the bond is. That is, how high or low is the probability that the company will default? Investors use these ratings as a guide to price bonds, based on the relative riskiness according to the ratings agencies.

The main classification that investors need to worry about in corporate fixed income is the distinction between investment-grade bonds and high-yield bonds. High-yield bonds are sometimes referred to as "junk bonds," defined by S&P as having a rating below BBB-. Companies that have achieved an investment grade rating of BBB- or above are the most likely to pay back their investors, while companies that sit in the high-yield category can be expected to default on their debt relatively more frequently.

As an aside, the published ratings on fixed income investments have come under fire at different points throughout history. In the Great Financial Crisis, "AAA" ratings (the highest possible) were given to some fixed income investments that eventually proved to have significant underlying issues and a much higher probability of default than was implied by the ratings. This is a stark reminder to investors to always bring a healthy dose of skepticism to the table.

Nowadays, average investors are less likely to buy individual bond issuances, which typically have higher minimum investment sizes and may not be traded as easily as stocks or may not even be available for trade outside of institutional investors. Instead, individual investors can more easily and cheaply put money into a bond fund, which pools investor capital and purchases a portfolio of bonds from different issuers. (See the discussion of "Individual Securities vs. Funds" below, for more details on investing in funds.)

Preferred stock is a term for another subset of fixed income. Investors argue about whether preferred stock is really debt or equity. I find that depends on the perspective of the specific security holder, but I group them under the broader fixed income classification unless they have embedded convertibility options that are in the money (pardon my French). Preferred stocks usually offer a fixed dividend payment in perpetuity and have priority over common stock, should the business ever be liquidated or sold. In this way, they are "debt-like."

Individual preferred stocks from companies are usually easier to buy than individual corporate bonds are, because they have a lower price (a $25 par value is a standard amount, compared to the $1,000 par value for most bonds) and are most often listed and traded on national stock exchanges, such as the NYSE. Utilities, financials, and real estate companies are all large issuers in the preferred stock realm. Preferred stock may also be rated by one of the agencies.

Corporate Equities (common stocks):

Equities, common stocks, or just stocks for short are probably the sweet spot for most individual investors. Stocks represent fractional shares of ownership in a corporation, and owners of stocks (called stockholders or shareholders) are entitled to company profits over time, in proportion to their ownership percentage. Largely because of their more volatile nature and second-by-second price moves, individual stocks receive the lion's share of media attention. High-flying stocks that are appreciating (moving up) rapidly can capture public attention almost as fast as the most recent celebrity cheating scandal (I said "almost").

Stockholders have some of the biggest influence when it comes to the future direction of corporations because collectively, stockholders own the company and are responsible for electing representatives to serve on a company's board of directors. The board, in turn, hires a CEO and other executive officers to run the company and maintains oversight over key business decisions and functions. Companies interact with their stockholders by publishing quarterly and annual documents with their updated financial statements and by hosting periodic conference calls to give their investors a view into what is going on, from an operational and strategic perspective.

Stocks are widely available through online brokerage accounts, such as those offered by Charles Schwab, Fidelity, Interactive Brokers, or Robinhood. Institutional investors (professional fund managers, endowments, pension funds, etc.) typically trade stocks through the large investment banks: Goldman Sachs, JP Morgan, Morgan Stanley, Merrill Lynch (owned by Bank of America), and so on. Prevailing market prices —the prices at which buyers and sellers are willing to trade shares—can be found through brokerage accounts, newspapers, or popular financial websites such as Yahoo Finance, Google Finance, and Koyfin. The Stocks app on iPhones has a particular cult-like following.

While owners of stocks are entitled to their share of a company's profits, that doesn't mean that shareholders can ride up to a company's headquarters on a trusty steed and demand their share of the profits in cash (or else!). As elected officials and fiduciaries, company management teams and boards of directors collectively decide what to do with a company's profits, if there are any. They may choose to pay out profits to shareholders by issuing a dividend, which is a cash payment made to all stockholders based on the number of shares they hold. Or, they may decide to reinvest those profits in the business, in order to grow and produce incrementally more profits in the future. The choice is theirs.

Capital allocation decisions such as these can have massive implications for business values over time, just as these types of decisions can greatly influence outcomes for personal capital allocators on an individual basis. Analyzing a company's management team is therefore a key component of security analysis, as we'll see in more detail in the Active Management section.

Private Assets, Derivatives, and Other:

This fifth and final category is a bit of a catch-all. Private investments are anything that doesn't involve buying a security on a public exchange. Investing in private real estate (renting out or flipping homes, for example) is a common private investment category for the individual investor. Making an angel investment to jump-start a business venture would also be included.

A lot of investors may find their interests or talents more suited to private vs. public investments. However, my view is that for the majority of people, it makes more sense to start by building up some public market investments, either through funds or individual securities, before branching out into the private markets. Doing so has three benefits: (i) lower entry barriers in the public markets; investors today only need $5 or $10 to get started in the stock market, while private investments typically require far more initial capital; (ii) greater liquidity, which refers to the ease of buying and selling securities, due to their being listed on exchanges; and (iii) professional management teams, compared to private ventures that may be light on management talent.

I won't spend much time on derivatives in this book—that's an advanced investment topic, best left for another day. But in general, what I will say is that derivatives can be a helpful risk mitigation and hedging tool for investors when used correctly, although for most investors, dabbling in derivatives won't be worth the added effort, since successful investment outcomes can be readily achieved without them. Investing in derivatives requires real time and effort, to understand how the products operate and how profits and losses are realized; so, if you choose to explore them, be careful and do some homework before getting involved. Buyer beware.

Also, one's primary home is often called the biggest investment a person makes in their lifetime. This is true in many cases. So, we give it its own space. While it's not covered here in the Pure Investment Capital section, housing is covered in greater detail in a later chapter.

Individual Securities versus Funds:

For the foregoing five asset classes—except, to some extent, private investments—investors typically have the option either to buy individual securities (stocks, bonds, etc.) directly, such as buying 10 shares of Apple stock, or put their money to work in a fund, such as buying 10 shares of a fund that holds Apple stock alongside other investments.

There are benefits to investing in a fund. These include (i) efficient diversification, since you have access to an entire portfolio of securities by making one investment; (ii) access to specific investment strategies or assets that would otherwise be unavailable, such as buying a fund that invests in foreign stocks or certain commodities, like gold; and (iii) access to professional portfolio managers—in the case of actively managed funds— who have been trained in security analysis and other portfolio construction techniques and can search for investments with the highest expected returns relative to investment risk.

Buyers of individual securities, on the other hand, benefit from the flexibility of being able to own stakes in specific companies and can more acutely express an investment thesis by putting capital to work directly.

One thing I do want to warn against regarding fund investments is the notion that buying into a fund means the investor doesn't have to do their homework. While it is true that for fund investments, idiosyncratic company risks won't have as large an impact on returns, the investor is still making a judgment call about the attractiveness of the securities that in aggregate make up the fund. There are no free rides. Even an investment in the S&P 500 is a bet that the 500 largest American companies will continue to produce attractive cash flow in the future and that those cash flows can be purchased at a reasonable price. This has often proven to be true over time, but it isn't sacrosanct.

Pouring the Concrete for a Strong Foundation

Allocating Pure Investment Capital well involves several basic building blocks that every investor should understand, even if they plan on pursuing a more passive investment program or if they plan on having others manage their money for them. These portfolio construction concepts are crucial. After discussing these concepts, the more passive investor should have enough of a background to confidently build a portfolio that suits his or her needs, while the more actively minded investor will have a great starting point for the next section, on Active Management.

What's more, a more informed investor will be able to spot fraudsters and predatory financial salespeople a mile away, giving them time to mount a counterattack. When it comes to your money, ignorance is not bliss.

We will explore three building blocks of basic portfolio construction: (i) diversification, (ii) optimizing risk/return, and (iii) rebalancing.

Diversification

Our first foundation principal is diversification, which is really just a fancy way of saying: Don't put all of your eggs in one basket. No matter how much research or insight one has into a particular investing situation, something random or unforeseen can always come along and produce a bad outcome out of a seemingly good investment opportunity.

Earthquakes, pandemics, wars, new regulatory regimes, a step-function change in technology, or even the sudden retirement of a key member of a management team can all contribute to detrimental randomness impacting an investment. While most readers have likely heard of diversification and understand the eggs vs. basket concept intuitively, below is a slightly more systematic approach on how to implement this idea.

In order to safeguard against occurrences that could cause serious harm to their portfolios, sensible investors make an effort to hold different types of positions, because the earthquake that impacts the California real estate company probably doesn't hurt the large London-based software business or the smaller Florida-based manufacturer of garden gnomes and lawn flamingos. I call these different types "risk exposures." As we'll see, holding investments with different risk exposures makes our overall portfolio significantly more resilient, because outside factors tend to impact only certain portions of our investments, rather than the entire portfolio at once.

Building a well-diversified portfolio is like putting together an all-star softball team. We need tall people who can jump high, strong people who can throw far, short people who can run fast, clever people who are always in a good position, sluggers who hit home runs, and accurate hitters who always get on base. Plus someone has to be in charge of music in the locker room. All of these players have different skillsets—some are more similar than others—but taken together they form a well-balanced and championship-caliber team.

Note that there are some kinds of risks that do impact substantially all our holdings and can't be diversified away, including a deep recession or a financial crisis. These are called systematic risks, and their existence is one of the key reasons why we build up a war chest of opportunistic capital.

No matter what happens, your FDIC-insured cash can't be negatively impacted as long as the basic financial and government systems are still functioning (and if they aren't, we have bigger problems).

A key thing to keep in mind when thinking about risk exposures is the degree to which investments are correlated, meaning how closely they move together. For example, investments in the stocks of two California real estate companies could reasonably be expected to perform similarly over time (the correlation between their risk and returns is high), meaning that something unexpected that negatively impacts California Real Estate Company A is also likely to negatively impact California Real Estate Company B. Even though they are two different companies, taken together, they don't necessarily diversify a portfolio.

The goal of diversification is to find investments that have low correlations with each other but still offer high expected returns. To do this, we have to first isolate the main ways in which investments are correlated (the basic risk factors, or our "baskets") and then, second, build a portfolio that incorporates an attractive mix of these characteristics (i.e., allocate some eggs to each basket).

So, given the choice of different types of positions, or multiple egg baskets, which baskets do we choose, how many of them do we need, and how many of our "eggs" do we put in each one? And, do we scramble them or try for over easy? (That last one is a matter of personal preference. It has nothing to do with investing and everything to do with breakfast).

To answer, let's look at the main types of "baskets," or risk exposures, that exist. This is not an exhaustive list, but a great start in terms of the main factors that can influence investment returns over time.

First, let's go back to a risk exposure concept we've already discussed: asset class. Investments within the same specific asset classes are likely to be more highly correlated than are investments in different asset classes. For example, on average, government bonds are going to exhibit a higher degree of correlation with other government bonds than they will with equities. In the Rebalancing over Time section, we devote more time to asset classes. For now, please just note that a well-diversified portfolio is likely to include at least some exposure to different asset classes, although the degree of diversification is likely to shift quite a bit over the life of the investor. For example, large concentrations of equity for a younger investor will likely give way to a more balanced stock and fixed income portfolio down the line.

The second type of risk exposure on the list is company size. Numerous academic studies analyze differences in the correlation of investment returns between companies of various sizes, with size typically measured by something called "market capitalization." Market capitalization, or "Market Cap," for short, represents the total value of the equity or stock outstanding for a particular company. It is found by multiplying a company's share price by the total number of shares outstanding. Another way of looking at market cap is to say that if one were able to buy all the stock of a certain company, the market cap is the aggregate amount that they would have to pay to own the company 100% (in addition to any net debt that the company has).

When you hear financial reporters or journalists make comments such as "Apple is a $2 trillion company," what they are typically referring to is the fact that Apple's market cap is roughly $2 trillion. (Trying to figure out how Apple got to a $2 trillion market cap and whether they can get to a $4 trillion market cap is precisely the type of subject we aim to unpack in the Active Management section.)

Winning the award for simplest framework in investing, the most common breakdown of company size with regard to market cap is just small, medium/mid, and large. The classifications vary a bit, but small cap companies typically have a market cap below $3 billion, while mid-cap companies may have a market cap from $3 billion to $30 billion, and large cap companies may be everything over $30 billion. Sometimes, investors will get even more granular and reference "mega cap" companies with market caps of greater than $100 billion, or "micro cap" companies with market caps of less than $100 million.

One shortfall of market cap is that it ignores the debt that a company owes. Some companies have no debt, while others have large amounts of debt, which can impact the perceived size of the enterprise. That's something to keep in mind, especially when looking at smaller companies with large amounts of debt. Total Enterprise Value is another metric frequently used by investors to measure company size. It incorporates debt by adding it (net of cash) to a company's market cap, among a couple of other adjustments.

Company sector, or industry, is a third key risk factor. The North American Industry Classification System (NAICS) codes provide a handy reference for classifying companies into industry groups. Businesses that operate within the same sector are more likely to be influenced by the same set of underlying business conditions. This makes intuitive sense. For example, we'd expect companies that derive a large portion of their revenue from the single-family home market to be influenced by changes in homeownership levels and housing affordability proportionately more than a company that makes chewing gum is (I haven't been able to discern any concrete differences between homeowners and renters in terms of who chews more gum. Study to follow).

When it comes to sector analysis, thinking about the end markets and ultimate drivers of demand for a company's products or services can be helpful both in evaluating the company's prospects and in thinking about diversification.

For example, car dealerships are involved with the actual selling of cars, auto manufacturers with the design and assemblage of the vehicles, automotive marketing agencies with crafting a story and figuring out how to define a target audience, and component suppliers to the auto manufactures are involved with producing certain key parts and systems for the car. Individually, these business models are very different (encompassing, distribution, design, engineering, creativity, and manufacturing), and so an investor may be tempted to view a portfolio holding these different types of companies as sufficiently diversified. However, the demand for cars is clearly the key driving force (pun intended) behind the revenues and profits for each company involved in the auto supply chain. So, these companies are not sufficiently diverse, with regard to the company sector risk factor.

Rounding out this list, our fourth key risk factor is geography. Companies that concentrate their business in a certain geography are likely to see a higher correlation of business fundamentals than those in other geographic areas, because their business will rely on local supply and demand dynamics. This is especially true for industries that don't export a large proportion of their products or services. Real estate is a great example of a localized industry. The office market in Dallas, Texas, isn't likely to have much to do with the office market in Tokyo, Japan, other than a general reliance on interest rates, the global business cycle and inflation expectations in each country. We can expect that two office landlords in Dallas will exhibit higher correlation in their businesses than do an office company in Dallas and one in Tokyo.

Investors often break down their portfolio exposure according to whether their holdings are domestic or international, because it allows them to control for factors such as differences in interest rates, GDP growth, personal incomes, taxes, political regimes and more. These differences lead to varying risk and return profiles for each investment. U.S. investors further delineate their international exposure according to developed versus emerging markets. These classifications are relatively simplistic but are still helpful to keep in mind. As with the company sector risk factor, thinking about end markets is helpful. Is the company in question a localized business such as the office landlord we mentioned, selling its services to those based in Dallas or Tokyo, or is it a truly global business such as Microsoft whose Office and Azure users span multiple continents? Companies often break out their geographic exposure by revenue in their annual filings or periodic presentations.

To summarize, the key risk factors (or investment types) include:

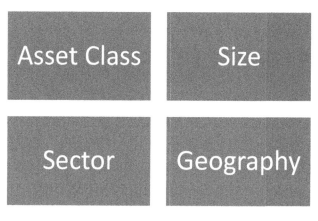

Figure 4.8: Primary risk exposures.

Putting this all together, we can see that in the foregoing example of two comparable California real estate companies, there is quite a lot of overlap in risk exposure: the investments share the same asset class (equity), operate in the same sector (real estate), share the same geography (California), and may or may not be similar in size. Punch line: Even if we owned a portfolio with 100 positions in the stocks of different California real estate companies (assuming this was possible), it would be foolish to think that this was a diversified portfolio, due to the overlapping risk exposures, which drive potentially powerful correlations between the companies. Unlike Mr. T, in finance, people don't pity the fool!

Now, how does knowledge of these risk factors translate into our first foundational investment principle, diversification? That is, how do we put these concepts into practice?

A prudent investor should aim to build a portfolio based on different groupings of these risk factors. Doing so effectively is a lot like getting an ice cream sundae with unlimited scoops. A kid in an ice cream store with access to unlimited scoops will be one of the best capital allocators you can find. The right balance of chocolate, vanilla, Phish Food, and mint chocolate chip is all you need for a delicious meal (some might debate whether an ice cream sundae is a meal. Some might not).

Sure, you could add in Rocky Road, but that's pretty close (and highly correlated) to Phish Food, so on the margin it doesn't benefit you much. Sure, you could get one of every scoop in the store, but that's probably too much ice cream, and all the flavors are going to melt together into "blah." Investors need to take a good chunk of each of their favorite flavors to find success long-term. This multifaceted optimization problem shows up time and time again in investing.

The size of each portfolio "chunk" is going to vary significantly, according to the financial resources and goals of each individual investor, but common sense will go a long way here. As a starting point for portfolio diversification, investors may also find the following "rule of three" helpful. The rule of three works as follows: ignoring asset classes for a moment, we are left with sector, company size, and geography as the three primary risk factors. The rule of three would be that for a well-diversified portfolio, investors should aim to get exposure to three different types of risk within each of these three primary risk factors. "Getting exposure" could be defined as allocating at least 10% to each type of risk.

Here's an example, to illustrate. Consider the first primary risk factor: sector. A starting point for a well-diversified portfolio would be to have at least 10% in each of three different sectors (say, real estate, technology, and consumer staples). Likewise, there should be at least 10% of the portfolio invested in each of the small, mid-cap, and large-cap designations. Finally, at least 10% should be allocated to three different geographic regions.

Figure 4.9 presents a summary of these risk factors. Note that these risk factors aren't mutually exclusive—i.e., there's overlap, meaning one could theoretically achieve adequate diversification based on the rule of three with just three equally weighted stocks: a small cap real estate company based in the United States, a mid-cap tech company based in Europe, and a large-cap consumer staples company based in Asia.

[Example Risk Exposures]   Goal: Aim to have at least three types of investments for each risk exposure

Sector	
Real Estate	25%
Technology	40%
Consumer Staples	35%
Total	100%

Size (market cap)	
Small Cap	15%
Mid Cap	15%
Large Cap	70%
	100%

Geography	
United States	60%
Europe - Developed Markets	20%
Asia - Emerging Markets	20%
	100%

Figure 4.9: Potentially diversified portfolio based on the rule of three.

Sometimes, investors think of diversification as being the ownership of a large number of investments. The key distinction I want to point out in this context is that it is far more helpful to understand the underlying risk factors likely to impact portfolio returns over the long-term. A 5- or 10-

position portfolio could be more diversified than a portfolio with 50 or 100 positions, depending on the underlying risk factors.

Asset class diversification is likely to be significantly influenced by one's age and financial status, which is why I left it out of the rule of three example. A younger investor with a longer time horizon is likely to hold a significant amount—perhaps all—of their Pure Investment Capital in stocks, while an older investor who is closer to retirement will have shifted over time into more fixed income positions. Depending on one's risk tolerances, our investor may choose to hold more or less of their assets in less volatile or more volatile positions; but having at least a small portion in each of the asset classes outlined is a good starting point.

Optimizing Risk versus Return

Pouring the Concrete: Concept #2. Our second foundational investing concept is to optimize risk and return when choosing investments. This is touched on at the beginning of Phase 3. If diversification can be boiled down into "don't put all of your eggs in one basket," then "optimizing risk versus return" can be equally simplified by the statement: "Pick from the best options available." As we shall see, optimizing risk versus return is about weighing the pros and cons of each prospective investment, to ensure that the investment goes as far as it can to help us achieve our goals.

While the interplay between the expected payoff if things work out (the return potential) and the potential for loss or an unexpected outcome (the riskiness) can be complicated, it is crucial to try and understand. Analyzing this relationship means factoring in different information, to arrive at a buy or sell decision for the position. The further we can go in optimizing the attractiveness of our positions, the better our long-term investment results will be, and the faster our wealth will accumulate.

To get started, let's check back in with Jordan, the factory worker in Phase 2. The last time we saw Jordan, he was posting sepia-toned pictures of the factory floor on his blog. Let's assume he's moved on from that activity. Like many of us, Jordan finds himself at the supermarket on a Sunday morning with $100 to spend and the task of buying enough groceries to last him and his pet chihuahua, D'Artagnan, for the entire week. Jordan has a taste for flavor and is also a bit of a health nut, meaning he won't be satisfied or able to meet his health goals by just buying bottom of the shelf products for his meals, in order to spend the least amount possible. Jordan has a multifaceted optimization problem to solve: he needs to meet his goal of buying groceries for the week, and get the most bang for his $100 bucks, while continuing to live a healthy lifestyle. Plus, let's not forget the seemingly insatiable D'Artagnan.

Jordan's task is very similar to the challenge faced by investors as they try to sort between different investment options that they hope will help them meet their long-term goals. Each decision involves some element of getting closer to the goal (earning a return) but also brings uncertainty about how it will turn out (risk) and must be accomplished with a limited set of resources.

Consider the cereal aisle. Jordan can't decide between his trusty Grape Nuts at $4, the supermarket's brand at $3.15, or a new, gourmet, organic Grape Nut-esque cereal that's been imported from Brazil and costs $6.50. How can he possibly choose? Sure, he could play it safe and go with the Grape Nuts, but would he be better off buying the cheaper supermarket brand and saving the $0.85 difference? They don't taste quite right, but it's only a week so maybe it is worth it. On the other hand, Jordan already saved $2.50 in the cheese department with a buy-one-get-one free coupon, so perhaps he should treat himself to the Brazilian blend? It costs more, which is risky, because he's never tried it, and it might not suit his tastebuds.

Jordan knows that if he buys the more expensive brand and it doesn't work out, then he will experience regret. This constant balancing between the cost, benefit, and uncertainty of different choices captures the investor's challenge succinctly. As we'll see, the job of the smart investor is to hone his or her decision-making process as it relates to risk and return, to reduce any stress associated with making important financial decisions, as well as to enhance the outcomes of those choices over time. All that and a bag of chips (assuming they fit in the budget).

As a rule, we want to find investments where we can earn the greatest amount of return while taking the least amount of risk. When choosing between two investments, if they offer the same potential return, then buy the less risky one. If they are the same amount of risky, buy the higher returning one.

If buying the expensive Brazilian Grape Nuts costs Jordan $2.50 more, but they taste amazing and it gives him $3 worth of satisfaction, he made a good investment. He bought something with a $3 value for the price of $2.50. He didn't know they were going to taste $3 better ahead of time though, which introduced risk, so he had to rely on his research and clues to make an informed guess about the probability of this cereal tasting $3-worth. Importantly, he eventually had to make a decision on whether or not to roll the dice. At the store, Jordan is trying to optimize for his nutritional health and happiness. In the investing realm, we are mostly attempting to optimize for long-term, low-stress wealth creation.

Whether investing in an individual stock or bond, buying into a specific fund, or even making a choice about whether or not to give money to a certain financial advisor, optimizing the risk/return equation means trying to understand which factors are likely to positively influence the investment (the key drivers of the investment thesis), the potential outcome of the investment if things go as planned (our reward for a satisfactory outcome), and the probability or likelihood that things turn out the way you are expecting (what are the chances?). In addition, we need to understand what could go wrong, assess the probability of something going wrong, and even account for the general uncertainty of outcomes (that is, "knowing what we don't know").

Collectively, this analysis concludes in our view of the risk/return offered by a particular investment. Choosing investments with the most attractive risk/return relationship is how we can improve the overall success of our portfolio. If this all sounds a little abstract at the moment, the method of reaching our goal here should become clearer as we progress with this section.

Returns:

We can start by quantifying returns. Usually, when we talk about returns, we are referring to the percentage profit achieved on an investment. So, if we invest $100 and one year later have $110, then the return that we earned is 10% ($10 profit divided by the $100 initial investment, over the course of the year). Expressing returns this way is helpful because it allows us to compare different investment options. For example, if I told you that you could invest $50 and earn a $5 profit, or invest $200 and earn a $30 profit, the easiest way to decide which was the better deal would be to note that in the first option you earn 10% ($5/$50) while in the second option you earn 15% ($30/200). Assuming that coming up with the $200 isn't a problem, we should prefer that second option, because it results in a higher rate of return and is therefore more optimal. 15% is better than 10%.

For the same reason that thinking about percentage returns helps us compare options, putting things in the context of an annualized return also helps us control for differences in the time horizon of the investments. For example, would you rather earn a 5% return in six months or an 8% return in one year? Assuming we could reinvest in these options multiple times, then we should prefer the 5% return in six months, because after six months we could turn right around and make the same investment again. By the end of the year, we'd earn 5% twice, for a total return of 10% (ignoring compound interest for a second), clearly preferable to—i.e., more optimal than—the 8%-in-one-year option. Higher returns equal more money.

Say Jordan is looking at high yield savings accounts instead of Grape Nuts and sees three options from three different banks that offer a 1.0% interest rate, 1.25% or 0.75% respectively. He should take go with the 1.25% account assuming the banks are all reputable and FDIC insured.

Understanding the source of our returns, or exactly how we derive profits, is just as important as understanding the actual percentage returns themselves, because doing so tells us what to look for in an investment, how much confidence to have, and also gets us thinking about some of the risks involved in achieving our goals. For the purposes of this book, we can break investment returns into two primary categories: (1) income returns, and (2) capital returns. Taken together, income and capital returns form the total return we expect to earn on an investment.

Income Returns

The first category, income returns, represents periodic payments distributed on an investment that provide a relatively stable yield on capital. In other words, income returns are interest or dividends paid to us over the course of time. The interest income on a bond, interest on a savings account, and dividends on a stock are good examples of income returns. So is earning rental income from that underground treehouse you list on Airbnb.

Bonds come into play quite a bit during the next few pages. Here's how most bonds work. To raise money, a company, government, or other entity issues a type of investment contract called a bond that says they promise to pay a certain amount (known as "face value" or "par value") at some date in the future (known as the "maturity date") and with a certain amount of annual interest in the meantime (known as the "interest rate" or "coupon"). Many times, when discussing bonds, investors refer to par value instead of face value, even though they essentially mean the same thing. In return, for this promise, the borrower gets cash from investors.

For most bonds, face value is $1,000, while the interest rate the borrower promises to pay depends on market forces (supply and demand). So, if Apple decides it wants to raise $1,000 and pay it back in five years, it could issue a bond with a $1,000 face value that matures five years from now. If similar companies have issued five-year bonds like this at a 4.5% interest rate, then Apple will likely offer a 4.5% interest rate on its bond as well. So, the face value is $1,000, the interest rate is 4.5% and the maturity date is five years from now. The last piece of the puzzle is the trading price. Most bonds are tradable between investors once issued. The market price of the bond is based on supply and demand. Typically, bond investors refer to bond trading prices as a percentage of par value. So, a bond trading at 80 means it is trading at 80% of par value (or $800 assuming par is $1,000).

For instance, a government bond that pays a 5% coupon will be expected to provide us with an income return of 5%, assuming we bought it at par (100 cents on the dollar). If we buy $1,000 worth of these bonds that mature in one year, then one year from now we will have $1,050. Let's say another one-year government bond was available that had a 7% coupon. From an investment standpoint, we could improve our portfolio by selling the 5% bond and reinvesting the proceeds into the 7% bond. We will have increased our expected return by doing so to the tune of an extra 2% per year.

But what if there was a bond yielding 10%, issued by a manufacturer of rectangular hula hoops? Should we sell our 7% government bond and buy the one with the higher income return? As noted earlier in Phase 3, the higher the risk of default on a bond, the higher the yield and expected return will be. Notice how risk is already bleeding into our conversation on returns. Understanding how to answer this question—the tradeoff between higher expected return and more risk—is the key goal of this section.

Like bonds, stocks may also offer investors an income return by way of dividend payments, which are periodic cash payments that companies distribute to their shareholders. A company whose share price is $100 and which pays a $3/share annual dividend will be said to have a dividend "yield" of 3%. This is an income return.

Unlike bonds, however, stock investors will not have as much confidence that they will earn that same 3% yield in future periods. This is because, while bond interest payments are contractual and set in stone at the outset, dividend payments on stocks are decided on by company boards of directors and management teams, and therefore could change frequently. Good companies with profitable businesses tend to increase their dividends over time.[24] On the other hand, struggling companies may

---

[24] That said, many good companies have attractive options for investing in their core businesses and may decide to do that instead of paying out cash to their shareholders with a dividend.

find themselves forced to reduce, or cut, the dividends they pay out. Overall, dividends on stocks are less sticky than interest payments on bonds.

As we'll see, income returns are easier to conceptualize than capital returns are, because income returns are generally stated in tangible terms at the outset of investing (the percentage coupon on a bond, the percentage dividend yield on a stock, etc. is known in advance). The most important things to analyze when assessing income returns are the probability that the company will be able to maintain these periodic payments, and the possibility, in the case of stocks, of payments going up or down in future. Again, this involves analyzing risk.

Each of these factors is heavily influenced by the profitability of the company or government that issued the security. Strong companies and governments tend to pay off their bond investors in full and on time, while weak ones may default and fail to make interest payments. Meanwhile, profitable companies maintain and grow the dividends they pay to shareholders as cash flows grow, while struggling companies may have to cut their dividend payouts.

Capital returns

While income returns refer to periodic payments over time, capital returns (sometimes called "returns on capital") relate to changes in the principal or investment amount when we sell a security, or let it mature, in the case of a bond. This is the other way investors try to profit from their positions.

As a real-world example, if you were to buy a house for $300,000 and rent it on Airbnb, you would earn periodic cash flow (an income return) by letting guests stay there, but if someone really wanted your house and offered you $400,000 for it, you could earn a capital return by selling it for $100,000 more than you bought it for. Depending on the situation, investors may prefer to invest for a capital return instead of an income return, or vice versa.

The familiar "buy low, sell high" doctrine is an example of earning a positive capital return. Generally, capital return means changes in the underlying security price during the holding period. Say we buy a stock at $50 and sell it at $75. We've earned a capital return of $25, or 50% (=$25/$50). Likewise, buying a bond at 90% of par value and holding it until it matures at 100% of par will result in a capital return of 11% (10 profit divided by 90 purchase price).

As was the case with income returns, analyzing the capital return potential of a bond is a bit more straightforward than it is for a stock, because the face value of a bond is contractually set from the get-go. If Jordan buys bonds at less than par, say 90 cents on the dollar for a bond with a face value of $1,000, then he has invested $900 (90% of $1,000) and can expect to earn a positive capital return—in this case equal to $100 ($1,000 - $900)—simply by holding until maturity. On the flip side, if D'Artagnon buys a bond at above par (say, at 105 for a total investment of $1,050), he can expect to earn a negative capital return—in this case, -$50 ($1,000 - $1,050).[25] Par value for the bond is a very clear representation of what we will get paid at the end if the investment goes as planned, which makes calculating the potential capital return simply a matter of comparing the price we are paying in the market relative to par value.

---

[25] One might ask why anyone would pay more than par value for a bond. This happens relatively frequently, however, in the case where the coupon on the bond is abnormally high relative to what one could earn in the market today. So, a bond issued five years ago that pays a 10% interest rate (an income return) is valuable in a market where all other bonds only offer 5%. Hence, investors might bid up the price of this 10% bond to above par.

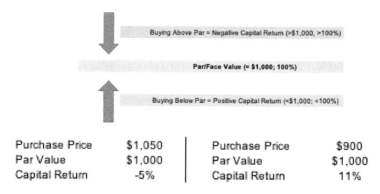

Figure 4.10: Bond prices relative to par and capital return outcomes.

When it comes to capital returns from stocks, though, the situation becomes more complex. Outside of certain situations,[26] stocks have no set maturity date or face value on which to base estimates. It would be like asking someone how much they think they will be able to sell their house for in five years. They can make an educated guess, but they don't know for certain. Instead, stock investors are tasked with figuring out where the stock price is likely to go in future periods relative to where it is today, which raises the million (or trillion) dollar question: What makes stock prices go up or down?

A Random Walk to the Stock Exchange

Entire books, nay, entire libraries have been written about what makes stock prices go up or down over time. Investors have been pondering this question since the creation of stock markets themselves. Today, many investors deploy an arsenal of analytical (and sometimes astrological) techniques to try and predict the future direction of stock prices. Other

---

[26] Such as a merger or takeover where the offer price of the stock is fixed.

investors take the stance that stock movements are completely random—in the short term, the random camp seems to have a point.

As usual, I'm going to keep things simple here. For our purposes, changes in stock prices over time—i.e., capital returns—are driven by two factors: (1) changes in the underlying intrinsic value of the company, and (2) changes in the price-to-value relationship.

First, let's look at intrinsic value, which is a concept that was popularized by Ben Graham, widely considered the architect of value investing. Intrinsic value relates to the underlying business value of a company in question, which can be thought of as the price that a buyer would pay to own the entire business. The intrinsic value concept means that regardless of what a company's stock price is doing at any moment in time, each company has a true underlying worth, based in large part (but not exclusively) on its current cash flows, the prospect of growth or reduction in those cash flows going forward, the level of interest rates prevalent in the economy and other factors.

The notion of what constitutes intrinsic value is similar to how we judge purchases in our everyday lives. When buying a car, we often ask: What is this car really worth to me? What advantages and disadvantages are offered by purchasing this particular car? Are there other brands or models I should consider? What did I pay for my last car, which was of similar quality? Thinking about purchases in terms such as these is very similar to conceptualizing intrinsic value, where we try to uncover what the valuable components of a company are. Alternatively, if no stock price were available for a given company, what would you pay to own a share?

Equally important as the concept of intrinsic value is the effort to understand the future path —or direction—of that intrinsic value. Simplistically, is the company going to increase its worth or decrease its worth over time? This comes down to fundamental analysis and probabilities, which are things we dig into in more depth down the line, but which readers likely already have a pretty good handle on.

Some questions that might come to mind are: Is this company going to be around in five years? 10? 20? What advantages and disadvantages does it have, relative to its competitors? Will the company be able to raise prices when it needs to, or will it have to make do by increasing the volume of goods or services it provides, and do we think they will be able to do that? How big are the markets in which the company operates? Have there been any changes in regulation that might increase or decrease demand for the company's products or services? These are just some of the questions that influence a company's intrinsic value.

In the back of our minds, when trying to answer these questions, it can be helpful to gut-check ourselves by assigning a probability to the chance that a particular outcome will occur. This is the framework that Annie Duke masterfully illustrates in her book, *Thinking in Bets*. Will the company be successful at entering a new geography? Would you make a bet with someone about it? If we think there's only a 10% to 20% chance of this happening, we should factor that into our analysis. Will a competitor dethrone our favorite in one of its core product areas? If the probability of yes seems like 70% or higher, we need to be aware of that.

I introduce basic ways to estimate intrinsic value in this section, but the bulk of that exercise is held back until the end of Phase 3, which is a more advanced discussion of security analysis. Understanding the concept of intrinsic value is crucial to every investor—not least because it lowers the chances that we overpay for an investment - but an extremely detailed and precise estimate of intrinsic value isn't necessary. Just as we don't have to know exactly how much a rock weighs to know that it is heavy, we don't have to know the exact intrinsic value of a company to know it is cheap or expensive.

According to my framework, the second component of what drives capital returns for stocks is market prices relative to intrinsic value. After all, the price you feel is fair to pay for a new car isn't necessarily the price you will be quoted by Beatrice, the salesperson at your local dealership. Depending on the supply and demand for the car you want, the time of the year, and what Beatrice ate for lunch that day, you might see wildly different prices quoted for the same car, even though your view of the fair price doesn't change.

The stock market is no different—prices can and often do diverge from what you think represents intrinsic value. This is where the market and its daily gyrations factor into the picture. This is often called the price/value relationship because it relates the price of the stock on the market today with our estimate of the company's true underlying intrinsic value. For example, if a stock is trading at $90, and we think it is worth $100, we'd say that the stock is trading at a 10% discount to intrinsic value, or that it has a price/value ratio of 0.9x ($90/$100). For every stock out there, we could theoretically come to a conclusion on whether or not the stock is trading at a discount, at a premium, or in line with its intrinsic value. This is a really helpful thing to look at because, over time, we would expect most stock prices to converge to the underlying intrinsic value of the company. As savvy capital allocators, we can guide our money to investments with the most favorable price/value ratios in anticipation of this.

As Ben Graham says:

> *In the short run, the market is a voting machine but in the long run, it is a weighing machine.*
>
> *The Intelligent Investor*

Let's try to shed some light on the workings of the price/value relationship with an example.

Suppose you are evaluating two publicly traded lemonade stands. The stands are exactly the same: they have the same equipment, brew batches based on the same recipe and charge the same amount per cup. They are also both located in the same market and are run by twin robots from the same manufacturer. Each lemonade stand produces $10 per year in earnings and has 10 shares outstanding, meaning that earnings per share is $1 for each business. Now, let's say further that the market price of Stand A is $20/share, while the market price for Stand B is $30/share. And finally, let's say that other lemonade stands in the public markets have traded for 25x earnings on average, throughout history.

Lemonade Stand A **Lemonade Stand B**

Lemonade Stand A			Lemonade Stand B		
Annual Earnings	$	10.00	Annual Earnings	$	10.00
Total Shares		10	Total Shares		10
Earnings Per Share	$	1.00	Earnings Per Share	$	1.00
Market Price Per Share	$	20.00	Market Price Per Share	$	30.00

P/E Ratios of Other Public Lemonade Stands:

Lemonade Stand C	24.0X
Lemonade Stand D	25.0X
Lemonade Stand E	25.0X
Lemonade Stand F	26.0X
Average:	**25.0X**

Figure 4.11: Two publicly traded lemonade stands.

Now that we've set the stage, we're ready to ask: Would you rather own Lemonade Stand A or Lemonade Stand B, and why? And, which has a better chance of improving its price/value relationship? After a moment of pondering, it should start to become clear that Lemonade Stand A is a much better buy. After all, investors are obsessed with getting the most bang for their buck and would much rather buy $1 of earnings for $20 than for $30 (saving that $10 difference to go buy some actual lemonade, perhaps). In investing parlance, we would say that Stand A trades at 20x earnings, while Stand B trades at 30x earnings. If all else is equal, lower earnings multiples mean better value for our investor.

Another tidbit from the example is that, on average, other lemonade stands have traded at 25x earnings. Assuming no large differences in quality between these stands, this should lead us to believe that there is a reasonably high chance that over the long term, the prices of Stand A and Stand B should both converge to this average, and therefore, would both be trading at $25/share. Using this valuation method—called "comparables," because we compare the stock values of companies under consideration to the values for other public companies—we'd conclude that the intrinsic value of both Stands A and B is $25 per share. Hence, Stand A trades below its intrinsic value by $5 ($25 - $20) and has a price/value ratio of 0.8X ($20/$25), while Stand B trades above its intrinsic value by $5 ($30 - $25) and has a price/value ratio of 1.2X ($30/$25).

Take note of this conclusion, because the essence of what we just said is that Stand A has a good probability of seeing its price to value relationship improve by the stock trading closer to its $25 intrinsic value. On the flip side, because of where Stand B is trading in the stock market, we would expect its price to decline over time until it gets to that $25 intrinsic value. Thus, the probability of Stand A's price/intrinsic value ratio appreciating (becoming more favorable) seems high, while the probability of Stand B's price/intrinsic value ratio deteriorating (becoming less favorable) also seems high. We are much more likely to earn a positive capital return by buying Stand A.

This is just one example of how to compare current trading prices to intrinsic value. In practice, though, things quickly become get more complicated. For example, what happens if we now consider two stands that operate in different markets—one in Times Square, in New York City, and one in a small town outside of Minneapolis? Maybe Stand A is using older equipment, which doesn't allow it to increase capacity as quickly as Stand B, which has the newest lemon juicer on the market. Such elements will influence our estimates of intrinsic value and therefore our conclusions about how attractively valued a company may be.

Buying stock in a company with a trading price below our estimate of intrinsic value is known as investing with a "margin of safety." The margin of safety principle is a bedrock concept of the strategy of value investing, but it may have different meanings to different investors. Regardless of whom you ask, however, almost all investors will agree that the higher the margin of safety, the greater the probability that we will make money on the investment. A strong margin of safety means that we feel good about the capital return side of our investment.

Total Returns, the Yin and the Yang

We've looked at two primary ways that investors earn returns on their money: income returns and capital returns. Each source of return comes with its own idiosyncrasies, but taken together, they form the complete picture of investment returns: what we call "total returns." So, a bond that pays a 5% income yield[27] and is trading at 90% of par value would have a

---

[27] Readers more familiar with bond lingo might note the use of "income yield" vs. "coupon payment" for our discussion. Coupon payments and percentage coupons refer to the stated annual payment on the bond as a percentage of face value. So, a bond with a 5% coupon might pay $50 of interest on a $1,000 of face value. Our use of income yield is akin to something called "current yield," which is the annual coupon divided by the *market* price of the bond. Hence, if this bond paid a $50 annual coupon and was trading at $900 (90% of par), then it would have an income yield, or current yield, of

prospective income return of 5% and a capital return of 11% (100/90), if the bond matures in one year. The total return, on an annualized basis, therefore, would be 16% (5% income return plus 11% capital return). This 16% is what we would expect to earn if we invested in the bond for one year. Generally, we try to state returns using an annualized percentage basis. Total returns are just the income return and capital return added together, which is an approximation, admittedly, but close enough for our purposes.

Likewise, a stock that we buy at $200 per share, which pays a 4% dividend and is expected to trade up to its intrinsic value of $250/share in one year, would have an income return of 4% and a capital return of 25% ($250/$200), for a total expected return of 29% (=4% + 25%).

Each investment has a component of income or capital return, even if that component is a zero, as is the case for stocks that don't pay dividends. The weighting, or proportion, of those income or capital returns differs, depending on the investment. Bonds typically offer proportionally higher income returns relative to capital returns because they pay a fixed coupon, while stock investments are often heavily skewed toward capital returns. As mentioned, some stocks don't even pay dividends and so may have an income return of 0%, leaving all of the investor's return to be made up of capital return.

After calculating potential total returns, investors must decide whether they are attractive. As we'll see, risk comes into play in a big way for that decision. But other factors, such as long-term savings goals, alternative investment options and many others, could influence the decision.

5.6% (=$50/$900). The percentage coupon on a bond mostly will be stable throughout the bond's life. The income yield, however, will change, depending on the market price of the bond.

A thorough understanding of these different sources of making money should allow the reader to more concisely weigh the attractiveness of investments they consider. This is a good segue into thinking about risk.

Risk

We've discussed risk a fair amount already in this book. Any time that a potential outcome has a less than 100% probability of occurring, there is a chance that a different outcome will actually transpire. Without risk, our investment decisions would be simple: choose the investments with the highest expected returns. Risk complicates the picture because it means we can't count on always achieving the returns we expect. Sure, the 10% yield on that rectangular hula hoop manufacturer looks juicy, but what if the round-hip population are the only ones who like to hula hoop? The company may go bankrupt, and we'd be left with a potentially worthless bond and no 10% return. Savvy investors learn to analyze the different kinds of risk in an investment and choose which ones they are comfortable with, and which should be avoided.

Many people understand risk management in the real world but are perplexed by the concept of risk in the financial world. I've known folks who rush to apply sunscreen in the summer, for example, so they don't risk burning, and who always check the weather before going outside in the winter, to make sure they are dressed properly (and don't risk freezing); but these same people will take a flyer on a new semiconductor supplier they've never heard of, because it seems like a quick way to make a buck. When it comes to investing, conservative decision-makers who carefully weigh changes in their career and in the saving aspect of their lives may engage in reckless speculation. As I say in this book, understanding the common-sense decision-making frameworks we employ in our own lives and translating that into investment activities is bound to improve outcomes.

For our discussion of risk, I tend to focus on the kinds of risk that will cause us to fail to reach our long-term return requirements. If we need 8% annualized returns to get that retirement funded, then we want to minimize the probability of earning something less than 8% annualized. Based on the foregoing discussion of returns, we now know that the two primary components of total returns are (1) income returns and (2) capital returns, and that for capital returns in stocks, the key drivers are (i) changes in intrinsic value and (ii) changes in the price-to-value relationship. Taking things a step further, to factor in risk, is really just another way of asking: What are the chances we will earn those returns?

For example, consider an investment in a heavily income-return focused security: a bond that yields 5% and is trading at par (100 cents on the dollar). In this case, the expected return is 5% and will come entirely from the income we receive periodically from the company that issued the bond. In thinking about risk here, the key thing to analyze is the probability that the company will continue to make those interest payments. If the company gets into trouble—because it overextended itself by taking on too much debt, or if the profitability of its core product or service deteriorates—then there could be a decent chance that it won't pay its bond investors. The higher this chance, the less good we should feel about buying the bond.

Likewise, let's think about a more capital-return focused security: a stock that pays no dividend (has an income return of 0%), is trading at $80 and has an intrinsic value of $100. Over time, we would expect the stock price in the market to reflect that intrinsic value: If the price moved up to intrinsic value today, we would earn a capital return of 25% ($100/$80 - 1). But there is a risk here that the intrinsic value declines or that it was never worth $100 to begin with (i.e., that our analysis was faulty). If the new venture that Company X was investing in doesn't pay off, or if a key relationship with Company X's largest customer falls apart, then it is likely that intrinsic value will come down from $100. If intrinsic value goes to $50 for example, then we bought something at $80 that is worth $50; in other words, we'd expect to lose $30 as the stock declines from $80 to $50, or 37.5% of our initial investment. This might not happen, but it could, and we as investors need to recognize the possibility.

Likewise, even if we end up getting intrinsic value correct, and the stock is worth $100, if we buy it at $120 we could still lose because of a deterioration in the price/value ratio.

My savvy readers are likely already piecing together my conclusion on risk, which is that analyzing risk means first really understanding the businesses we are investing in and then not overpaying for those businesses (i.e., not paying much above intrinsic value). We want strong, profitable companies that will grow their cash flows in the future, or even perhaps less strong companies that we can buy at a significant discount to intrinsic value. We want to avoid weaker companies whose best days are behind them. We may even want to avoid companies that are strong but where we would have to buy in at a price way above our estimate of intrinsic value. Sticking with the former and eschewing the latter is the key risk management effort that our reader must undertake.

Investors should really try to understand how the company under inspection makes its money. Who are the customers and what is driving their demand? Are there competitors who pressure your company to cut its prices or offer superior service for the same price? Does the company seem to be growing only by making acquisitions, or is there real organic business growth happening? Is the company taking on too much debt? What are the sustainable competitive advantages this company has? Do we expect this industry to be relevant in the future? We don't have to have answers all of these questions for each investment, but we should at least be able to write down what they key risk factors are that might cause our business to struggle, down the road.

In that vein, when evaluating investment risk, we are looking for circumstances that might cause a company's profitability to decline in the future. Too many of these risks point us to the conclusion that this is a bad company, or at least one with poor future prospects.

Over long periods of time, unless the price-to-value ratio is completely out of whack (as it was for certain tech stocks in the dot-com bubble, for example), then it is my view that focusing on the business fundamentals and evaluating investment risk will produce more than adequate outcomes when combined with a long term ("buy and hold") mindset. The price/value relationship is a bit less important when we are holding on for five years or more. In other words, make sure you aren't getting screwed out of the deal on valuation factors—that is, paying such a high price that even if the business makes money, you will lose on your investment—but otherwise, spend most of the time thinking about the underlying business and how it is going to look 3, 5, 10, or 20 years from now.

In summary, a thoughtful evaluation of the risks in an investment is key to long-term success. If return analysis is the way we determine how we win, then risk analysis is how we minimize the chance that we lose. Defense wins championships.

Applying this risk/return mindset to fund investments

Even though the discussion of optimizing risk/return has focused on individual stocks and bonds so far, the same concepts apply to investments in funds. Investors should understand the attractiveness of a fund's

155

strategy, as well as what types of companies are included in the portfolio. Valuation metrics for funds (such as p/e ratios[28]) are often available, which can help investors gauge whether, on average, the fund's investments are trading above or below a reasonable estimate of intrinsic value.

One thing to consider when investing in funds, rather than in individual securities, is that fund investments involve an extra layer of fees, to compensate whoever is managing the fund. These fees can eat into performance over long periods of time. For example, if a fund earns 10% annual returns before fees and pays a 1% fee to the manager, then investors are giving up 10% of their profits (1%/10%) to the manager. Just as in evaluating the risk/return characteristics of a particular security, the investor should examine the fund's strategy, track record, fees and risks, to make sure they are going in with their eyes wide open.

Mutual funds and ETFs are subject to regulation that mandates adequate disclosures to current and prospective investors, meaning that researching a fund shouldn't be too hard. Before investing in a fund, it would be a good idea to at least read through a description of the strategy, look at the top holdings (investments), understand the key risk factors and evaluate the fund's fee structure. Sometimes the underlying holdings in the fund can be a surprise, compared to the name of the fund, which is something to watch out for. In this way, so-and-so's Robotic Future Fund might be filled with companies whose main business is to produce movies about robots, and the top holding of that Space ETF might have more to do with space heaters than outer space exploration. It always pays to look

---

[28] A p/e ratio—more formally known as a price-to-earnings ratio—is a common investing metric found by dividing stock price by a company's earnings per share. It shows how much an investor would have to pay to buy a dollar of earnings. If a company has $10/share of earnings, and its stock trades at $100/share, we would say that the stock is trading with a p/e multiple of 10x. Higher multiples mean that a company's earnings are seen as more valuable, while lower multiples imply the opposite.

at the top holdings before buying a fund; this information should be widely available.

My comments about funds can be extended to the practice of evaluating outside advisors as well. Even when delegating your capital allocation decisions to someone else, it pays to understand how they plan to invest. Where does the advisor plan to park your money? Are they optimizing for income returns and periodic cash flow, or trying to grow capital over time? What kinds of risks are they comfortable taking? How are they being compensated? Do we get any free pens when we go to the office? (Ballpoint pens are a particular favorite). The same analytical mindset we've been using all along can be applied here.

Rebalancing

A few years after we caught up with Jordan in the supermarket, he and D'Artagnan have met a woman (who had her own pet chihuahua, named Sprott), and decided to settle down and start a family (of humans or dogs; they haven't come to a conclusion). They also want to buy a house (again, for humans or dogs; we can't be sure). Hence, in a few short years, Jordan's financial profile and goals have evolved considerably. He probably needs to look at rebalancing his portfolio, to accomplish his new objectives.

Jordan's updated situation is a great segue into our third category of fundamental investing concepts: rebalancing. Rebalancing means adjusting one's portfolio from time to time based on changes in life circumstances, or changes in underlying position sizes, relative to targets. Most of what we talk about with regard to changing life circumstances results in changes to asset class allocations, for example, shifting from stocks to bonds. Changes in position sizes relative to targets—for example, going from 15% invested in tech companies to 25%—have more to do with the sector, geography, and company size factors discussed earlier, in the diversification section.

Changes in life circumstances are a constant feature of, well, life, but also of investing. These changes impact our financial context and shape what the right set of investments may be for any given situation. For example, when Jordan started out in his career, his income and expenses were most likely at a low point relative to what they will be in the future. He may or may not have had student debt to cope with, and his savings were probably minimal.

As Jordan moves through life, however, these initial circumstances will morph into something different. He, his partner, his dog, D'Artagnan, and the canine-in-law, Sprott, may move to a new city with a different cost of living. He may be promoted or move into a higher-paying job at a different company. Later on, he may get married or have children or decide to start a small business. Regardless, throughout all of this, he will gradually be moving closer to eventual retirement and will need to finance that. As a smart capital allocator, he needs to update his investment strategy amidst these changes, to keep himself best-positioned to meet his objectives.

Rebalancing Due to Aging

Aging is probably the biggest change in life circumstance that most people will encounter. Understanding the financial implications of aging is important because, for much of our lives, aging correlates positively with average earnings and expense levels. That is, they all tend to go up over time. In addition, as we age, the time horizon we have to invest before retirement shrinks. Over longer time horizons, we might feel safe investing most of our assets in a broad selection of equities, to take advantage of the higher returns that equities tend to provide, relative to other assets.

However, over short periods of time, we can't be as certain we will achieve those higher returns. It takes adding to a portfolio across multiple economic and market cycles to benefit from these long-term advantages.

One central concept in rebalancing is that as most people age and approach retirement, they will want to shift away from equities (or stocks) and toward a higher proportion of fixed income (corporate or government bonds or preferred stock). Younger investors who are just starting out and have a long time horizon can make use of the fact that on average, equities have outperformed bonds. In shorter time horizons, however, equities can be volatile; the returns might be lower than for bonds and could very well be negative.

In other words, as the time horizon shrinks, the ability to withstand large fluctuations in stock returns, relative to bonds, diminishes, as does the probability of earning the historical return on stocks. This is the law of large numbers in action: Over many years, investors who have broad exposure to the market can reasonably expect to earn something close to the historical return on stocks (in the 7%–12% range, depending on when and how this is calculated), while over shorter periods, their returns may differ materially from this average. If you need the money now, you can't wait until the market recovers. Once Jordan is within a few years of retirement, his ability to take large risks declines because he doesn't get the benefit of averaging out over several market cycles. D'Artagnan is going to have to reel in that portfolio of early-stage biotech companies he's been putting together.

In addition, many retirees rely on their investment portfolios to produce stable income, a feature of almost all fixed-income investments, but one that is less common for stocks (which may or may not choose to pay out dividends).

The key concept linking our discussion on changing circumstances with rebalancing is that time plays a central role in the ability to take risk.

This is why many investors reduce their stock allocations as their time horizon shrinks, preferring to invest proportionately more in corporate or government bonds, or other lower-volatility investments. One very rough heuristic I've seen quoted is to subtract one's age from 100 and invest the resulting percentage in stocks with the remainder in fixed income (either by buying individual securities or by putting money into funds). Therefore, a 20-year-old investor might invest 80% (100 - 20) of their portfolio in stocks and the rest in fixed income, while a 60-year-old investor might only invest 40% (100 - 60) of their portfolio in stocks, with the rest in fixed income. This example is a very simple system for rebalancing over time, according to changes in age, but I think it is directionally helpful. Of course, it is up to the individual and their risk preferences to decide how much to allocate to fixed income—that's exactly why we spend time in this section developing the skillset to make those kinds of choices.

As an aside for those looking to earn more consistent, bond-like returns but without locking themselves into a low rate (the 10-year Treasury pays 2.8% at the time of writing, not exactly a juicy return), private or publicly-traded real estate may be an attractive alternative, especially if the real estate in question produces stable long-term cash flows that are "bond-like." There are numerous public real estate companies that own high-quality portfolios of property and are managed by professionals. In addition, private real estate investment could be an interesting option for someone approaching retirement, as a way to fund their cost of living after they stop full-time work (and it could even provide a new part-time career, going forward).

Rebalancing Due to Changes in Revenue/Expenses or Other Life Events

Other life circumstances that bear monitoring are those that cause underlying cash flows to increase or decrease materially in a relatively short amount of time: a raise or new job that pays more, a rising or falling level of expenses, or changes in underlying goals, such as deciding to save up to buy a house or pay for an education. Having a child (or five) is another decision with significant financial implications. Each of these situations or changes should trigger a re-think of investment allocations, to make sure we stay on track.

In practice, rebalancing due to changes in cash flow or life events is similar to rebalancing due to aging, which is really just a way of rebalancing to fund the large, long-term goal of retirement. Changes in cash flow that boost savings, such as getting a raise or finding a new way to cut expenses, can result in a higher proportion of funds allocated to equities, while decreases in cash flow might prompt one to shift proportionately more of their portfolio to fixed income, to the extent that preserving principal and safety becomes a greater focus. If Jordan loses his job and is forced to rely on his investments to sustain himself, he probably doesn't want to be dealing with too much volatility and should "downshift" his risk.

Having some more money in our pocket means we can use that money to more aggressively grow our wealth, depending on how attractive the investment options out there are at a given time. Likewise, sometimes, defense needs to be prioritized because of a drop in savings. These situations ebb and flow in mostly unpredictable ways. Being successful in the long term means being flexible and willing to adapt. Again, noticing a change in life circumstances and using that as trigger for thinking about rebalancing is helpful. Do we want to play more offense right now, or more defense?

Outside of changing life circumstances, our second category of rebalancing is a result of responding to changes in our position sizes—meaning, what percentage of our assets we have in each investment—relative to our target. This kind of rebalancing need may surface due to appreciation or depreciation in the underlying positions that we hold (hopefully appreciation!), as well as due to changing investment theses, for example, waking up one day to realize that the portable waffle-shaped lunch containers made by Waff-2-Go aren't going to be the next iPhone-caliber invention.

As an example of this second kind of rebalancing in action, consider a $300 "equal weight" portfolio that has just three positions: 1/3 in a small-cap stock fund, 1/3 in a mid-cap fund, and 1/3 in a large-cap fund:

Portfolio	Value	%
Small-Cap Fund	$100	33.3%
Mid-Cap Fund	$100	33.3%
Large-Cap Fund	$100	33.3%
Total	$300	100%

Figure 4.12: Initial portfolio weights.

Let's say that this "1/3 in each" strategy is the optimal one for our portfolio's owner, based on his or her investment goals and thoughts about the market. Over the next six months, however, small-cap stocks break out to the upside in a big way, appreciating by 50%, while the mid-cap and large-cap portfolios stay flat. Six months from now, the updated portfolio would look like this:

Portfolio Update #1	Value	%
Small-Cap Fund	$150	42.9%
Mid-Cap Fund	$100	28.6%
Large-Cap Fund	$100	28.6%
Total	$350	100%

Figure 4.13: Portfolio weights, after the small-cap fund outperforms the mid- and large-cap funds

As a result of the move in the small-cap fund, our actual position sizes now vary quite a bit from the 1/3 in each targets that we believe to be optimal. So, we decide to rebalance to restore the original "1/3 in each" strategy. For a $350 portfolio, this would imply that each position should be worth ~$117 (=$350/3). Hence, we would need to sell $33 (=$150 - $117) of the small-cap fund and buy $16.50 each of the mid-cap and large-cap funds. The new, rebalanced portfolio would look like this:

Portfolio Update #2	Value	%
Small-Cap Fund	$116.5	33.3%
Mid-Cap Fund	$116.5	33.3%
Large-Cap Fund	$116.5	33.3%
Total	$350	100%

Figure 4.14: Portfolio weights after rebalancing

Note that there are costs to rebalancing (transaction costs, potential tax liabilities, psychological impacts, etc.), so allowing for a moderate amount of deviation from the plan shouldn't be a big deal and may even correct itself over time, without needing intervention from the investor. In Figure 4.14, this self-correction would look like the mid- and large-cap funds outperforming the small-cap fund over the next period, bringing the total portfolio closer to the "1/3 in each" equilibrium, without any intervention needed from the investor.

While periodic rebalancing is vital for investing success, one could probably take a slightly more lax attitude in managing position sizes relative to targets, to avoid what has been described in the investing world as "cutting the flowers while watering the weeds." In other words, if position sizes get out of whack because something in a portfolio is doing well, we may not necessarily want to cut it back just to reallocate our dollars to the other investments, which have been relatively weak. This is more art than science.

Also influencing the need to rebalance are changes in investment thesis. For example, if my new outlook is that the risk/return equation for public real estate securities is favorable, while the risk/return for airline securities is unfavorable, it would make sense to allocate proportionally more of my dollars to real estate and proportionately less to airlines. This is where the active manager can do his or her homework and start to improve their portfolio performance over time, by investing in line with their specific worldview.

To sum up the work in this section, when taken together, the building of a thoughtfully diversified portfolio, a focus on investments with the most attractive mix of risk and return, and the act of rebalancing over time should lead to a strong investment foundation and set the stage for stress-free investment adventures. This foundation is critical and, just like the foundation for a house, once this infrastructure is established, there isn't much maintenance work required. Adding to investments as savings come in and performing thoughtful risk/return and rebalancing analyses over time should be a "super-chill" way to build wealth.

Investors might find that the simplest way of implementing these foundational concepts is through dollar-cost-averaging into the market over time in a way that achieves the goals of diversification, optimizing risk/return and rebalancing. Dollar-cost-averaging just means periodically adding a set amount of money to investments. It is the autopilot of the investing realm. After going through the savings analysis and optimization in Phase 2, it should be clearer how much savings is available to flow into Pure Investment Capital, so taking that amount each month and allocating it according to these principals can automate the process. Dollar-cost-averaging helps smooth the ups and downs of investing in different economic backdrops as well, and minimizes the time spent thinking about business cycles and market timing.

Next, we dive deeper into the rabbit hole and see how more actively-minded investors aim to beat the averages.

Toolkit Summary—The Three Heroes Of Capital Allocation

- The Three Heroes give us a framework for translating our savings into the most useful areas. The Three Heroes are: Working Capital, Flex Capital, and Pure Investment Capital.

- Working Capital is usually the first stop for dollars coming in and is most likely composed of cash held in a checking account. Working Capital is crucial, but not a place to store too much excess money. Keep it tight (a few months' worth of expenses).

- Flex Capital is both a safety reserve and a war chest and is typically stored in a savings account. It should be larger than working capital, but the total size is fluid. Money stands ready to step up if there are changes in life circumstance and also if there are great investment opportunities.

- Pure Investment Capital is where the real action is in terms of passive wealth creation.

- The Third Master Formula states that Investments = Principal*Returns. This roughly translates to the future value formula: FV = Principal*(1+rate of return)^time. The Third Master Formula shows how a starting amount of principal grows into a larger amount over time. A higher rate of return means money grows faster. A longer time horizon means money gets larger.

- Returns are investment profits, typically expressed as an annual percentage.

- Risk means uncertainty about future outcomes. We can't always be sure that what we expect to happen is going to happen.

- Thinking about the combination of risk and return is how we decide if certain investments are attractive.

- Investors need to be aware of the impact of inflation as well.

- There are five asset classes (types of investments) to know about: cash, government debt, corporate fixed income, equities, and other (private assets, derivatives, etc).

165

- The concepts in the Pure Investment Capital section apply to individual securities, funds, and advisors.

- A strong investment portfolio makes use of several foundational concepts: diversification, optimizing risk/return, and rebalancing.

- Diversification means don't put all your eggs in one basket. The primary risk factors for diversification purposes include asset class, size, sector, and geography.

- Optimizing risk and return is all about choosing the best from the options available. Understand and maximize the different kinds of returns. Buying below intrinsic value is helpful here (a kind of margin of safety). Make an effort to think about the risks that could cause investments to fall short. Where is the portfolio most exposed? Are there company-specific, macro, regulatory, or alien invasion factors that could hurt us?

- Rebalance over time to adjust to changes in age or other life events.

Turning Things Up a Notch: Active Management

In boxing, we had Muhammed Ali. In investing, the undisputed heavyweight champion of the world goes by the name of Warren Buffett. As of the end of 2019, Buffett's primary investment vehicle, Berkshire Hathaway, has increased its stock price at roughly 20% per annum since 1965, while the annualized returns for the S&P 500 were roughly 10% during that same time period.[29] A shareholder in Berkshire Hathaway who had invested $10,000 in 1965 would have ended up with a portfolio worth a staggering $189 million, while an investor in the S&P 500 would have ended up with a $1.7 million portfolio (that's not shabby, but it pales in comparison to the Berkshire returns).

---

[29] Berkshire Hathaway 2019 Annual Report.

This track record is probably the best illustration of the benefit of active management, which encompasses any investment method that uses research or unique strategies to try and enhance risk-adjusted returns. Buffett, and those who bought and held Berkshire stock alongside him, was able to achieve that impressive track record by following a value investment mindset and concentrating his capital on companies that he thought would outperform over time. While not every investor will be able to compound his or her returns by 20% annualized for more than 50 years, my view is that by understanding the foundations of active management and savvy capital allocation, investors will be able to meaningfully improve the performance of their portfolios relative to an entirely passive approach. And, it is likely they will enjoy their investing experience quite a bit more by gradually honing their technique.

My own origin story with the stock market and active investing was through an antiquated device known as a print newspaper. My parents had discarded the finance section of the paper, and I began curiously combing through the tables wondering what all the different symbols and numbers meant. I wrote down a couple of the stock symbols as well as the numbers printed next to them (these were stock prices, as I came to learn later), and then performed the same exercise the next day to see which prices had changed. After this, I was hooked. A year or two later, my dad was courageous enough to open a joint custodian account for me to invest out of. With an eclectic portfolio of Nike, Abercrombie & Fitch, and Apple, I proceeded to lose $6 on my first day. It was devastating.

Luckily, I had the advantage of patient capital. Dad had forgotten his password so couldn't log in to see the losses—this may have saved my investing career! Also, my cousin Michael had been around the markets a while and helped show me the ropes. We will hear more from Michael in the Tax section.

The goal in this section is to arm the reader with enough analytical firepower to confidently approach any potential investment. A lot of what I described in the prior section, that is, the ideas of diversification across multiple primary risk factors, making use of several asset classes, looking for situations with optimal risk/return and rebalancing over time, should produce solid results on average for the readers of this book. This section is all about taking the concepts we presented before and turbocharging them with strong analysis, to find ways to increase the odds of earning above-average investment returns without taking on undue risk. This is the goal of active managers. Contrary to what some may believe, active management does not mean calling your broker while on the treadmill.

If learning about businesses, the economy and different investing strategies sounds like pulling teeth (assuming our reader isn't a dentist), then a more passive approach based on the Pouring the Concrete concepts should be enough to produce solid investment outcomes. However, if investing sounds like a fascinating thing to learn about (dare I say, something to sink your teeth into?), then a more active approach to learning and experimenting can really up the ante, in terms of potential returns.

Regardless of where a person feels their motivations lie, the processes and strategies in the Active Management section are highly important for analyzing investments or investment managers. Even a more passive investor, who mostly buys funds rather than individual securities, will still need to analyze those funds or analyze the adviser they are selecting.

What Kinds of Active Management Decisions Lead to Outperformance?

Let's start by illustrating some ways in which the concept of active management manifests itself. Consider the S&P 500 index at a high level. This widely followed group of 500 of the largest public companies in the United States has produced roughly 9% shareholder returns on average over the past 15 years. "On average" means that some companies in the index have done better than 9%, while others have done worse.

Well, if some companies have done better than the index, doesn't that mean we can just invest in those companies and be well on our way to investment riches? Not quite, unless you have a time machine and can go back 15 years to place those bets (in which case, you probably have some more interesting things to do than read this book). How do we make use of the knowledge that some specific companies are going to outperform the index over time and that concentrating our investments in these companies may allow us to beat the odds and increase our wealth at a faster rate?

The problem here is that what worked during the last 15 years isn't guaranteed to work during the next 15 years. The winners of yesteryear relative to the broader market may not be the winners of tomorrow. However, studying the existence of these winners (and what makes the greats "great") is useful when thinking about what drives the outperformance of investments, overall.

For example, a portfolio consisting of $10,000 spread evenly across Nike, Home Depot, and Microsoft, purchased in 2005, would have grown to roughly $80,000 in value by 2020, while a $10,000 investment in the S&P 500 would only be worth around $35,000 (ignoring the dividends in each case, which were roughly the same). This means that an investor in

NKE, HD, and MSFT would have made an additional $45,000 above what they would have made, had they kept their money in the S&P. Does this mean that investors took more risk, or got lucky by investing in Nike, Home Depot, and Microsoft? Does it mean that this same portfolio will beat the S&P during the next 15 years? The answers to those questions come down to the reasons for that outperformance, with business factors such as expanding cash flow, favorable industry dynamics, etc., as well as stock market factors such as the price/value relationship we spoke about earlier in the section on optimizing risk and return.

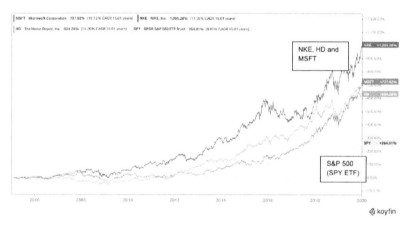

Figure 4.15: Relative returns of NKE, HD, MSFT, and the S&P 500®
(proxied by SPY ETF).

Source: *Koyfin*.com

Active investors try to use various techniques to shift their portfolios toward these above-average opportunities—not just in the S&P, but throughout the entire investable universe. I believe that these efforts can pay off over time, in the form of stronger investment results, as well as a more interesting and enjoyable investing experience. But we must start by recognizing that for any period of time, by definition, some investments will beat the market, while some will not.

Many techniques that active managers employ involve an in-depth analysis of a company or industry, with the goal of developing a differentiated viewpoint on the attractiveness of the security in question. Usually, if we are buying a security for the long-term, this means finding a situation where the current market perception of a company is worse than the underlying reality.[30] Maybe General Electric just missed a few quarters of earnings relative to analyst expectations, which caused the investment community to sour on the company and sell the stock (driving its price down). If we think that cash flows at General Electric are likely to rise materially in the future, we might make an active decision to load up on shares before the pessimistic investor community catches up.

Opportunities might also arise from recognizing a trend early. For example, if we happened to live by or visit one of the first Shake Shacks that opened and noticed the lines cueing up down the street for its irresistible patties, we could take that observation to the stock market to buy shares before the investor community wised up.

Sometimes, factors like complexity, size or geography can lead to great active management opportunities. Companies going through a restructuring may be too complicated for the average market participant to look at, for example, leading to underpriced securities. Small market cap companies may not even be investible by the larger fund managers, and with fewer eyeballs paying attention, mispricing can occur. Even much larger companies can be significantly influenced by the sentiment of market participants at a given time, which may not match up with the investor's long-term outlook for the company. Knowledge of a specific geographic area can also be a key competitive advantage in the search for outperformance (especially in sectors like real estate). Paying attention to qualitative factors such as management changes, strong customer reviews

---

[30] If you are shorting a security, it would be the opposite.

on a new product, or a change in the competitive dynamics in an industry that haven't flowed through yet into cash flows for the companies involved can also be lucrative places to search for opportunities.

What's more, the individual investor has some great advantages in the market relative to other participants, which can increase the likelihood that their active management decisions lead to favorable outcomes. Individuals aren't constrained in their timelines and don't have clients or colleagues pressuring them to make decisions. They can choose to invest when they want, in whatever quantities they can afford to, and in whatever securities they fancy.

The individual is also not constrained by liquidity. For the most part, if they find a security they like, they can buy it without too much trouble. This isn't the case for larger investors, who may be running funds that are too big to be able to buy into smaller companies without moving the price or owning too much of said company. If a fund manager oversees $5 billion in assets, she isn't going to take the time to underwrite a $200 million company. Even if she could buy 10% of that company, it would only represent a $20 million investment, which is less than 1% of her fund ($20 million/$5 billion). Not worth the trouble. But this isn't the case for most individuals.

Individual investors can also benefit from being outside of the faster-moving ecosystem of professional investing and can take their time, lining up investments for the long-term without worrying about short-term performance or gyrations in the market.

Applying the Active Management Mindset

Applying the mindset of active management means aggressively searching out interesting investment opportunities, analyzing those situations according to qualitative and quantitative criteria and then coming to a conclusion and acting on it.[31] For our purposes, there are three primary stages to an active management process: (i) idea generation, (ii) analysis, and (iii) execution.

Figure 4.16: Investment process for active managers.

Idea Generation

Why do your friends keep buying Yeti coolers? Why do you suddenly want to own one? Wait, aren't they a public company? Maybe worth a look?

That's a credible example of the idea generation process. There are others. More generally, there are two primary methods for generating investment ideas: the top-down approach and bottom-up approach. Within each method, there are numerous channels to tune into, to locate attractive opportunities.

In the top-down approach, investors try to identify broader economic, societal, or sector trends and then apply those conclusions to specific investment opportunities. In short, top-down idea generation starts with critical thinking about broad changes and whittles those thoughts down into actionable investments.

For example, maybe investors foresee a widespread return to fame for bell-bottom jeans. A quick Google search for the largest bell-bottom jeans

---

[31] Note that "acting on it" could mean doing nothing—there can be great value in perceived laziness.

manufacturers and brands reveals that Bellhop's Amazing Denim (fictional, but descriptive) is one of the largest, and you are in luck: Bellhop's Amazing Denim is publicly traded. You've just generated a lead from a top-down observation about fashion trends.

Other examples of investment leads from top-down thinking might include families moving to the suburbs from urban areas, cloud computing continuing to win share of IT budgets, inflation picking up in the future, economic growth in India surpassing that of other developing nations, or manufacturing and installation costs for solar power declining over the next five years. The key with top-down thinking is "skating to where the puck is going," in terms of where investors see the world going and then matching that worldview to specific investment opportunities.

By contrast, the bottom-up approach starts with a specific investment opportunity and evaluates it according to the security analysis principles we detail below. For example, investors might run a stock screen to identify companies trading at a 52-week low, meaning that the stock prices for these companies are at their lowest point in the past year (signifying the potential for undervalued securities). Maybe one of the companies recently had a management change or introduced a new product that is starting to gain traction in the market, which could represent a turnaround opportunity that hasn't been priced into the stock yet. That's an example of bottom-up analysis: We come across a specific security, analyze it, and figure out that something interesting and unique is going on with the company.

Many investments combine elements of both bottom-up and top-down idea generation. An interesting company often draws the investor to a new industry that they hadn't considered before, only to realize that there are some favorable industry tailwinds that haven't been fully appreciated by the market. Or, investors come to a conclusion about a broad change in society, or in a particular industry, which leads them to three or four companies poised to benefit, at which point, individual bottom-up analysis would likely ensue.

Top-down or bottom-up ideas can come from a variety of channels. Stock screens—in which investors input parameters and generate a list of companies or securities meeting those parameters—are a good place to start. Newspapers, trade journals, conversations with investors, and a "hunter" mindset of using the eyes and ears (and maybe smell?) to ferret out underappreciated stories can all produce interesting opportunities to beat the market. Over time, investors develop a better intuition for the kinds of companies or opportunities that are likely to produce real, actionable ideas. As always, patience and some good old common sense go far.

Idea generation is all about being curious, casting a wide net and then learning to recognize some of the factors that lead to promising investments. After all, we only have so much time in the day, especially if investing isn't one's primary occupation, so we need to train ourselves to quickly decide whether to dive in on a new idea or to pass for now and look for something else. This decision-making framework is one of the key skills that active managers try to develop, and it forms over years of analyzing companies using concepts like the ones we will discuss below.

One last thing to note about idea generation is that once investors start to plug themselves into the investing universe, they may quickly find themselves inundated with stock tips. Sometimes it can be hard to tell when someone is trying to give you a stock tip. But, if you feel as if you're being sold something—and that something is a can't-lose investment opportunity—that's a pretty good sign that someone is hawking you the latest and greatest stock tip. A good rule is to run in the opposite direction. That said, investors are constantly tapping their network of colleagues to source ideas, so building up a group of people whom you trust and who share in the same analytical, grounded framework that you do can be immensely helpful for finding and analyzing companies.

Analysis

Idea generation is a critical starting point, but the journey doesn't stop there. Buying an idea without doing the follow-up analysis is like buying a house without doing an inspection. It may look great from the pictures online, but that doesn't matter if the previous owners installed an inter-dimensional wormhole in the basement.

The correct depth of analysis will vary with every investor and each investment, but at the very least, I feel that investors should do some research into the following areas: company creditworthiness, company and industry outlook, price to value relationship, and management team. As in prior sections, our discussion assumes the point of view of someone looking at the equity or debt of a particular company; however these comments generally also apply when evaluating funds or financial advisors.

Creditworthiness

Examining creditworthiness is a fancy way of asking questions like: Can this company pay its bills and is it likely to be able to keep paying its bills in the future? Does this company have too much debt? Are the underlying assets that this company owns of high-quality? Are there large expense items in the future—operating losses, new product introductions, acquisitions, etc.—that are going to suck up cash and put the company on a risky footing?

Banks carry out a similar analysis on you when you are looking to buy a home. How much debt are you looking to borrow, what kind of job do you have (and how stable is that income stream) and have you borrowed in the past or failed to make good on any of your commitments?

Replicating this analysis for investments involves answering many of the same types of questions.

Understanding creditworthiness is one of the most important things to get right when investing. In short, strong and creditworthy companies tend to survive, while misjudging a company's creditworthiness can lead to actual bankruptcies—very much an example of a permanent impairment of capital. As Warren Buffett has aptly described it, "anything times zero is still zero." By "zero" he means bankruptcies—stocks can be wiped out in that case, leaving investors with nothing.

Companies borrow in a variety of ways, some straightforward, such as issuing bonds or taking out a bank loan, and some not as straightforward, such as buying inventory on trade credit, leasing assets, or being in an industry that has high levels of fixed costs (so-called "operating leverage"). Entire books could be (and have been) written about analyzing company creditworthiness, but for our purposes, let's focus on two things: the amount of debt that the business has relative to its assets (similar to a loan-to-value ratio on a home), and the level of operating income relative to debt service costs such as interest expenses (similar to a debt service coverage ratio).

In terms of the first point, the amount of debt relative to assets, investors should make it a point to examine at least the net debt to enterprise value ratio, which is explained below, using Proctor & Gamble as an example. Net debt just means the total amount of debt that a company has, minus the cash they have, as theoretically this cash could be used immediately to pay down debt.

Net Debt = (Total Debt) - (Total Cash)

Take a look at Figure 4.17, which shows Proctor & Gamble's balance sheet,[32] and see if you can locate the total debt and total cash. Done? The cash is found at the top of the table, labeled "cash and cash equivalents" and is equal to $10.288 billion. Meanwhile, debt is separated into two parts, debt due within one year, equal to $8.889 billion, and long-term debt, equal to $23.099 billion, for a total debt of $31.988 billion. Hence, net debt is equal to $21.7 billion (= 31.988 - 10.288).

Consolidated Balance Sheets

Amounts in millions except stated values; At of June 30	2021	2020
Assets		
CURRENT ASSETS		
Cash and cash equivalents	$ 10,288	$ 16,181
Accounts receivable	4,725	4,178
INVENTORIES		
Materials and supplies	1,645	1,414
Work in process	719	674
Finished goods	3,619	3,410
Total inventories	5,983	5,498
Prepaid expenses and other current assets	2,095	2,130
TOTAL CURRENT ASSETS	23,091	27,987
PROPERTY, PLANT AND EQUIPMENT, NET	21,686	26,692
GOODWILL	40,924	39,901
TRADEMARKS AND OTHER INTANGIBLE ASSETS, NET	23,642	23,792
OTHER NONCURRENT ASSETS	9,964	8,328
TOTAL ASSETS	$ 119,307	$ 120,700
Liabilities and Shareholders' Equity		
CURRENT LIABILITIES		
Accounts payable	$ 13,720	$ 12,071
Accrued and other liabilities	10,523	9,722
Debt due within one year	8,889	11,183
TOTAL CURRENT LIABILITIES	33,132	32,976
LONG-TERM DEBT	23,099	23,537
DEFERRED INCOME TAXES	6,153	6,199
OTHER NONCURRENT LIABILITIES	10,269	11,110
TOTAL LIABILITIES	72,653	73,822
SHAREHOLDERS' EQUITY		
Convertible Class A preferred stock, stated value $1 per share (600 shares authorized)	870	897
Non-Voting Class B preferred stock, stated value $1 per share (200 shares authorized)		
Common stock, stated value $1 per share (10,000 shares authorized; shares issued: 2021 - 4,009.2, 2020 - 4,009.2)	4,009	4,009
Additional paid-in capital	64,848	64,194
Reserve for ESOP debt retirement	(1,006)	(1,080)
Accumulated other comprehensive loss	(13,744)	(16,165)
Treasury stock, at cost (shares held: 2021 - 1,579.5, 2020 - 1,529.5)	(114,973)	(105,573)
Retained earnings	106,374	100,239
Noncontrolling interest	276	357
TOTAL SHAREHOLDERS' EQUITY	46,654	46,878
TOTAL LIABILITIES AND SHAREHOLDERS' EQUITY	$ 119,307	$ 120,700

Figure 4.17: Proctor & Gamble's balance sheet, as of 6/30/2021.

Our first metric, net debt to enterprise value, is found by dividing net debt into total enterprise value, which is a measure of what the company's trading value in the market is today. Enterprise value is found by adding

---

[32] Accessible from the SEC's website (www.sec.gov) or from the company's investor relations website.

net debt to market capitalization (share price times number of shares outstanding) plus non-controlling interest. The reason we look at this is because enterprise value gives us a more realistic view of how investors are valuing a company's assets in the market than we get by looking at total assets on the balance sheet, which is an accounting entry and less tied to reality. Financial websites such as Yahoo Finance or Google Finance report enterprise value. Proctor and Gamble's enterprise value is $365 billion at the time of writing. This is what the market is telling us it thinks the entire business is worth.

Dividing the net debt of $21.7 billion by the enterprise value returns 5.9% (21.7/365). We can think of the net debt/enterprise value ratio as similar to a loan-to-value ratio for a house. When we buy a house we typically put down 20%, which equals an 80% loan to value. In Proctor & Gamble's case, their loan-to-value is 5.9%, which seems reasonable. This paints a picture of a healthy company. Score one for Mr. Clean.

Net Debt/Enterprise Value = (Net Debt)/(Net Debt + Market Cap + Non-Controlling Interest)

When considering this metric, higher levels imply that more debt is being used to finance the assets of the business, which is generally a bad thing as it relates to creditworthiness. As debt levels rise, so does the probability that the company will be unable to pay its debts. For example, if total assets are 100 and net debt is 80, then the net debt/assets ratio is 80%. If assets decline 25% to $75 (which certainly wouldn't be unheard of in a recession), then the business is now underwater on its loans and is likely considered insolvent. That's bad news. It would be like owning a house worth $75k that had an $80k mortgage on it. However, if the business only had a net debt/assets ratio of 50% ($50 of net debt and $100 of assets), then the 25% decline in assets from $100 to $75, while painful, at least wouldn't lead to insolvency.

Note that in many companies, cash is greater than total debt. We call these "net cash companies," and they have among the strongest financial positions possible. Many tech companies are in the net cash camp.

After taking a peek at the net debt/enterprise value ratio, we can analyze cash flows relative to interest costs. This measures how much income a company earns relative to the amount it has to pay in interest on debt. There are multiple ways to calculate this, but to keep it simple, let's look at operating income relative to interest costs. This is often referred to as "interest coverage." Interest coverage is useful, because it gives the investor a sense of how easily a company can meet its interest payments.

Operating income consists of revenue minus operating costs. It doesn't account for interest payments yet. Most companies report operating income on their income statement as its own line item.

Operating Income = (Revenue) - (Operating Costs)

One can usually find a separate entry for interest expense below operating income. A higher ratio of operating income to interest expense signifies a large cushion, in terms of the company being able to meet its regular debt service.[33]

Interest Coverage = (Operating Income) / (Interest Expense)

In Figure 4.18, we look at Proctor and Gamble's income statement, to calculate interest coverage. P&G's operating income in 2021 was an impressive $17.986 billion, while the interest expense was $502 million. Hence, the interest coverage ratio is 35.8x ($17,986/502). This leaves us to believe that P&G has plenty of room to cover its interest costs.

---

[33] Some companies display interest expense as a negative number and some as a positive number on their financial statements. It depends on the company whether it shows up as ($100) or $100 for example. Either way, use the positive value for the sake of the interest coverage calculation. In other words, take the absolute value of the interest expense so as not to get a negative number for the interest coverage ratio.

Operating income would need to fall more than 95% for it to be below interest expense. A result like this corroborates what we already guessed by looking at the net debt/enterprise ratio: Proctor and Gamble seems to have a very strong financial position.

Consolidated Statements of Earnings

Amounts in millions except per share amounts; Years ended June 30	2021	2020	2019
NET SALES	$ 76,118	$ 70,950	$ 67,684
Cost of products sold	37,108	35,250	34,768
Selling, general and administrative expense	21,024	19,994	19,084
Goodwill and indefinite-lived intangible impairment charges	—	—	8,345
OPERATING INCOME	17,986	15,706	5,487
Interest expense	(502)	(465)	(509)
Interest income	45	155	220
Other non-operating income, net	86	438	871
EARNINGS BEFORE INCOME TAXES	17,615	15,834	6,069
Income taxes	3,263	2,731	2,103
NET EARNINGS	14,352	13,103	3,966
Less: Net earnings attributable to noncontrolling interests	46	76	69
NET EARNINGS ATTRIBUTABLE TO PROCTER & GAMBLE	$ 14,306	$ 13,027	$ 3,897
NET EARNINGS PER COMMON SHARE: [1]			
Basic	$ 5.69	$ 5.13	1.45
Diluted	$ 5.50	$ 4.96	1.43

[1] Basic net earnings per common share and Diluted net earnings per common share are calculated on Net earnings attributable to Procter & Gamble.

Figure 4.18: Proctor & Gamble's Income Statement for 2019–2021.

One important thing to note about creditworthiness is that debt levels are likely to vary by industry. All else being equal, industries that tend to produce long-term, stable cash flows—such as income-producing real estate, or utilities—are able to operate with higher levels of debt, while industries with volatile or negative cash flows—such as a startup technology company—would likely operate with significantly less debt or, preferably, no debt. Investors that want to go a step further could compare debt for the company under consideration to that of peers in their industry. Being an outlier in terms of using too much debt would not be favorable.

Also note that many free or low-cost investing websites report these and other useful metrics. Yahoo Finance, Seeking Alpha, Barron's, Koyfin, and Google Finance can be helpful places to look and are probably easier to navigate than the SEC's website (www.Sec.gov).

Credit ratings can also be a helpful indicator of a company's ability to pay its debts. Most large companies will be rated by one of the primary credit rating agencies: S&P, Moody's, and Fitch. A quick search of "{company name} credit rating" will probably do the trick there.

Overall, evaluating creditworthiness is about protecting against unforeseen financial stress that can lead to bankruptcy. Having an investment going to zero should be avoided at all costs. Historically, it has been hard for companies to go bankrupt without having much debt, although rapid industry shifts, catastrophic events, or outright fraud can always come into play.

A well-financed company is usually a sign of a conservative management team, as well, which can be looked upon favorably. Shareholders usually don't want their management team gambling with the long-term stability of the business by taking on too much leverage. Who would you rather let borrow your car, the person with a lead foot who tries to beat the light every time, or the one who prioritizes getting safely from A to B? If the lead-footed friend is Vin Diesel's character from *Fast & Furious*, this might be complicated to answer.

Company and Industry Outlook

After forming a view on creditworthiness, we can dive into analyzing the business prospects of the company in question and its broader industry backdrop. In the idea generation stage, investors are already thinking about companies and industries with an attractive outlook. Evaluating the company or industry as part of the analysis stage involves going deeper, looking at both qualitative and quantitative factors.

It might make sense to start with an examination of the industry. Are the products and services produced by the industry becoming more relevant or less relevant? Are there substitutes or competing technologies that could come out and disrupt the status quo, for example, e-commerce companies disrupting traditional brick-and-mortar retail? Are there many firms in the industry competing against each other with commodity products, which would likely make it hard for one specific company to succeed over the longer term? Who are the main competitors and what do they compete on—price, value, service, user experience, distribution? How fast is the industry expanding its revenue and what are forecasts looking like for the future? Are companies in the industry well-capitalized on average, or are debt levels high across the board? Is a rising industry tide going to lift all boats, or is a tsunami going to cause shipwrecks and bankruptcies? Does your CEO have any hidden dance moves?

After looking at the industry and its structure, investors can zero in on their specific investment candidate and see how it stacks up against the rest of the companies in that space. Favorable attributes could include a company that has a strong product lineup and large distribution footprint, or which has developed some proprietary technology that its competitors don't have. A large user-base or installed base could also be a competitive advantage.

Many investors use some version of the famous "Porter's Five Forces" framework in thinking about a company's competitive strengths. This analyzes how the company stacks up relative to its customers, who the company's main suppliers are, what competitors exist, what substitute products/services exist, and the likelihood that new competitors will enter the market.

When examining a company, keep thinking about what the special sauce is that is likely to cause this company to win over the long term. In fact, it might be a good idea to write down what the special sauce is for each company you invest in. If you are investing in a sauce or seasoning company, this becomes triply important.

Price to Value Relationship

Our third underwriting criterion is one that we've alluded to before: the relationship between market price and intrinsic value. As a refresher, market price is what the stock, bond or other instrument trades at in the public market—the price that investors would be able to buy or sell at by placing an order with their broker. Intrinsic value represents true underlying worth—the theoretical value that a buyer would pay for the entire business if they had access to perfect information and economic conditions were normal. One favorite saying I've heard about this concept is that price is what you pay, while value is what you get.

Examining the price to value relationship is all about coming up with an estimate (usually a range) for intrinsic value and comparing that to the current trading price of the security. If the intrinsic value is above where the security is trading, the security is said to be undervalued, while if the security is trading above the intrinsic value it is said to be overvalued.

Figure 4.19: Price/value relationship.

So, how do we calculate an estimate of intrinsic value? Seasoned investors use multiple different valuation methods and try to triangulate a range for intrinsic value. As with creditworthiness, entire books have been written about how to do this. We encourage anyone to explore these if they are interested. For our purposes, we'll introduce three primary methods.

The first two are based on comparisons between our company and other companies in the space, which is a type of analysis that many readers do every time they go shopping, with questions like: Why should I pay for the blue shirt from Macy's when I can find the same type of shirt for half the price at T.J. Maxx? Or, why should I pay $40 for this blue shirt when the one I bought last week was similar and cost $30?

The last method is a bit more esoteric but is how many professional investors value companies.

Public Comparables Method

Let's start with the public comparables method, because it is the most straightforward, given that most of us already use it when making purchases. For example, if our reader has ever found him or herself looking at the _Kelley Blue Book_ value for a car, or a Zillow "Zestimate" for a house, they have used a comparables strategy to value an asset. In both situations, similar cars or houses are grouped into categories based on common characteristics such as manufacturer, model and year (for cars), or square footage, geography, design, and year of construction (for houses). For investing, this method involves finding peer companies in the public market and comparing their trading prices relative to fundamental factors such as revenue or cash flow.

For example, consider evaluating a cybersecurity company for which we have identified 10 other publicly traded cybersecurity companies. If these 10 other companies trade at a 15x price/earnings ratio on average—meaning that their share prices are 15x as high as their earnings per share—then we can assume that a similar p/e ratio is reasonable for our company. Thus, if our company earns $3/share, a reasonable guess at intrinsic value would be $45/share ($3 of earnings times 15x P/E ratio). If the company's stock was trading at $30, it would appear to have a favorable price to value relationship, based on the public comparables method. This is because we have the chance to buy something for $30 that we estimate to be worth $45, which means we get $15 of value for free.

Transaction Comparables Method

The second valuation method involves looking at the history of acquisitions or takeovers in the industry and figuring out the multiples at which those transactions occurred. After all, if we are trying to figure out what a certain company would trade at in the private markets, it makes sense to examine actual transactions that have taken place over the past few years. The analysis for this method is similar to the public comparables method, except that instead of looking at other publicly traded companies, we are evaluating merger or acquisition transactions.

For example, if all the mergers and acquisitions of cybersecurity companies over the past five years have taken place at around 20x earnings, then all being else equal, we could assume that buyers are willing to pay 20x earnings for our cybersecurity company. This would imply an intrinsic value of $60/share ($3 earnings times 20x multiple). Again, were the stock to be trading at $30, it would seem to have a very favorable price to value relationship. Were the stock trading at $75, we might be a bit more cautious.

One thing to note on evaluating transactions is that transaction multiples include what's known as a "control premium." This is the amount of money that an acquirer will pay over current market value for a company, to gain control of that company. As a result, transaction comparables may produce intrinsic value estimates that are higher than those implied by the public comparables method. However, this could give a more realistic interpretation of the valuation that a buyer would put on a company, in order to take it private. Public comparables make use of shares trading on the open market each day, while transaction comparables make use of large, whole-company mergers and acquisitions. Analyzing from both angles can be illuminating.

For each method above, it is important to consider making directional adjustments to the multiples to account for differences in company or asset quality. For example, two manufacturing companies in the same industry might each be earning $5/share, however one company may have much newer equipment or substantial unused capacity, which would allow it to grow faster and generate higher margins. All else being equal, this likely means the company with newer equipment has a higher intrinsic value and should trade at a higher multiple of earnings. Many other factors could come into play that would shift a company's actual intrinsic value above or below what is implied by peer or transaction comparables.

Discounted Cash Flow Method

One key tenet of financial theory is that the value of an asset is equivalent to the present value of its future cash flows. Professional investors apply this to valuing companies by adding up all the future expected cash flows and discounting them back to the present, in order to figure out how much those profits should be worth today. Naturally, this is called a discounted cash flow analysis. Present value is a concept that we've touched on in past chapters. For our purposes in Phase 3, we'll take a slightly more comprehensive overview and defer to more advanced texts for a full exploration of the topic.

The concept of present value is that cash flows—money coming in or going out the door—have different values, depending on when they occur.

For example, say that I owed you $1,000 (what I did to be indebted to my readers aside). If I offered to pay you that $1,000 either today, in one year, or in 100 years, chances are that you would take me up on my offer to pay today. Why is that? Well, for someone receiving a cash inflow, the closer that inflow is to present day, the more valuable it is, because we can realize its benefits sooner. Finance professors and economists will be quick to tell you that a dollar today is more valuable than a dollar in the future, because that dollar held today can be invested and earn a positive rate of return. Likewise, a dollar one year from now is more valuable today than a dollar 20 years from now because of the option to invest, and so on.

More robustly, if we assume that the risk-free rate of interest (say, perhaps, the one-year yield on a government bond) is 5%, then one dollar today can be invested without risk and will be worth $1.05 (=$1 + 5%) a year from now. This works in reverse as well, although it can be a little harder to interpret. Namely, $1 one year from now would be worth $0.952 today (=$1/(1 + 5%)). Recall the compound interest formula discussed in prior sections: FV = Principal*(1 + return)^time. When we move forward through time, using principal to calculate future value, we multiply by (1 + r)^t, where r is the rate of return and t is the time in years. But when we move backwards in time, using future value to calculate starting principal, we divide by (1 + r)^t. That's present value in a nutshell. So, we can say that a dollar one year from now has a present value of $0.952 at a 5% discount rate.[34] The parallels to the compound interest formula exist because each formula is describing the same process of how money moves forward and backward through time.

---

[34] When doing a present value calculation, interest rates are typically referred to as "discount rates," because we are taking a value in the future and discounting, or reducing, it to a value in today's terms. Investors strongly enjoy making up new synonyms for interest rate.

The concept of present value comes into play with company valuations through a technique called discounted cash flows (DCF). A DCF analysis involves estimating the future cash flows that a company will produce that can be used to pay investors, and then discounting them back to today, using the present value math just described.

In theory, this should give us the intrinsic value of the company since we've accounted for all the future benefits that the asset (i.e., the company) will create, and we've presented them in terms of that value today. In practice, however, it can be difficult to estimate cash flows over even the next three years, let alone throughout the rest of a company's life. But there are numerous techniques and different kinds of sensitivity analyses that can be used to help produce a more accurate estimate.

For our purposes, I think the thing to take away from this is that DCFs can be an extremely useful tool in the valuation arsenal, especially when dealing with a company that has stable and predictable cash flows. All else equal, companies that produce higher cash flows today are more valuable than companies whose cash flows are smaller and expected to come further out in the future. That said, always be cautious of relying too much on the assumptions plugged into a DCF model.

When we combine each of the three valuation techniques—public comparables, transaction comparables, and discounted cash flow models—we should be able to triangulate a reasonably accurate view of a company's intrinsic value. Depending on where the stock is trading today, this might imply that the shares are undervalued, overvalued, or somewhat reasonably valued.

As discussed earlier, buying securities below their intrinsic value increases the probability of a successful investment outcome. When we pay $10 for a security that we think is worth $20, then we only lose money if our estimate of intrinsic value is off by quite a bit and the stock is ultimately worth less than $10. The lower the purchase price relative to our estimate of intrinsic value, the lower the probability that we will lose money in the long run, if our analytical framework is sound. On the flip side, there are situations where one can make money paying more than intrinsic value for something, but the odds are not on their side. And in terms of extremely overvalued situations (bubble-like territory), it usually pays to stay away.

Staying away doesn't mean giving up on the idea entirely, however. If the other aspects of the investment "check the box," then perhaps see if there is a similar company that will benefit from the same industry tailwinds but trades at a less expensive valuation, or if there is a cheaper security in the capital structure of the company you are examining. Can you earn a solid return from preferred stock that the company has issued? Can you take advantage of volatile changes in the share price to buy or sell options intelligently? Are there convertible bonds? Another route would be to wait things out and add the company to your watch list for the time being. Expensive stocks aren't always expensive, and there will likely be some moments in time when investors can establish a position at a more attractive price. Many investors keep a watch list of companies that they'd like to own if the price came down and set alerts to automate the tracking process.

Management

Our last due diligence item is to evaluate the company's management team. After all, these are the men and women running the company, and their decisions are likely to have huge implications for shareholder returns over time. There are many ways to evaluate a management team, but the key thing to zero in on is decision-making capability. Has the company been able to increase its market share by introducing innovative new products or services? That's pretty hard to do without a competent C-suite. Have the core business segments performed well, and do they continue to grow revenue and profits? Has the company made any strategic acquisitions or divestitures that have worked out particularly well or particularly badly? How has the stock price done? Have there been any key additions to the management team recently? Does the management team seem well-respected by the broader investor community?

Insider ownership by the management team and board of directors is a plus. If the CEO is also the largest shareholder, you can bet that she will do everything she can to increase shareholder value. On the other hand, if the CEO holds very little stock, takes a huge salary and bonus every year and flies around on the company jet while the stock languishes, we might have a problem.[35]

A company's press releases and transcripts—quarterly or annual calls with investors giving an update on the business—can be a good place to start when trying to evaluate a management team. Most big business decisions are accompanied by a press release where the management team explains the reasoning for what they are doing. It can be helpful to read these and try to understand why the company is using the words it is using and what kind of story it is trying to tell. Also, check to see if there have been any interviews with the CEO or other key officials. Company executives are often asked to participate in conferences or give television interviews, and these can be great ways to hear the story, interpret body language, and get to know the management team in greater depth.

Google away to your heart's content, to get a better picture of the people running your company, but remember that management teams are more likely to speak optimistically rather than point out the flaws in their business. As such, it is always a good idea to look for diverse opinions or try to track changes in management commentary across time. Examining actions rather than words—such as stock purchases and sales by executives

---

[35] A lot of this information is available in the company's proxy or Schedule Def-14A, which can be found at the SEC website: SEC.gov.

or other insiders, or resignations from key executives—can provide helpful context on what is going on inside a company.

Execute on the Investment Opportunity

After working through the analysis above, investors should have a pretty good understanding of whether they'd like to buy the security in question. Executing the trade is typically no more complicated than logging into an online brokerage account when the market is open—usually, Monday through Friday, from 9:30 am to 4:00 pm ET outside of holidays for U.S. markets—and placing an order to buy shares at the prevailing price. For larger companies that trade a lot of shares per day, investors can usually place what's called a "market order" to buy or sell, which means that the order will be executed at whatever the prevailing trading price may be.

However, if a security is thinly traded, meaning that not very many shares trade per day, then it is typically a good idea to place what's called a "limit order," which is an order to buy a security at a price that you specify. This is because for illiquid securities—those that don't trade often—your buy order may actually move the market price. Placing a limit order can help make sure that you don't accidentally pay a price substantially above what you were anticipating.

For example, if the market price is $10/share, and only 10,000 shares trade per day, for a total value traded of $100,000 (=$10*10,000), then our order for 1,000 shares may move the market price. It is 10% of the daily volume traded in one order, which in most situations would be considered a lot. This could move the market price up to $11 or $12, for example, before we are able to execute our entire order. In contrast, placing a limit order at, say, $10.50 per share would ensure that we don't pay more than $10.50 for any purchases.

Note that for new positions—especially in an unfamiliar industry—it is usually a good idea to start with a smaller position and then add to it over time, as one's conviction in the investment thesis builds. You never know how that pair of pants will fit until you've actually worn them (even if they were made by Bellhop's Amazing Denim); the same runs true for owning securities.

Once the buy decision has been made and the trade executed, investors can monitor changes to the business fundamentals over time and keep watch for competitive threats or other developments that could derail the investment. Setting up alerts—for example, through the company's Investor Relations page, or using a tool such as Google Alerts or the SeekingAlpha app—is a great way to passively consume updates about your portfolio companies. Public companies in the United States publish quarterly updates on the SEC's website (earnings releases and more expansive filings on forms 10-Q and 10-K), which are rich sources of information, as well as ad hoc updates (on another SEC document: form 8-K) for material business events that occur intra-quarter.

Knowing when to sell is equally important as knowing when to buy. Investors may sell for a multitude of reasons, but most of the time securities will be sold if (i) it turns out that the analysis was faulty, i.e., the company's position wasn't as strong as you thought, (ii) the fundamental environment changes—new competitors, bad management decisions, etc., (iii) the security price could be seen as substantially overvalued, to the point where future returns from owning it are highly likely to be negative even if the business performs well, or (iv) other portfolio management reasons, such as needing the cash for a more compelling opportunity elsewhere. A savvy approach to sales can add value to one's portfolio over time. For example, cashing out may allow you to capitalize on an overpriced stock, freeing up cash to fund another exciting investment opportunity.

Toolkit Summary—Active Management

- Active management is the jet fuel that can turbocharge portfolios.
- The active management process includes three stages: idea generation, analysis, and execution.
- Ideas can be generated from anywhere. Bottom-up or top-down thinking can be helpful in different situations. Be curious, read a lot and ask questions. Make use of any particular background strengths or diverse perspectives you have.
- Analysis is how we turn ideas into investments. The analysis stage is similar to researching and inspecting a house or car one wants to buy.
- Checking debt levels can help make sure there is very low bankruptcy risk in the investment. A shaky financial foundation doesn't take much to crumble.
- Evaluate the strengths and weaknesses of the company, and think about where the industry is going (a horse and buggy business could look great, but doesn't work if cars are the future).
- Analyze the price to value relationship using either public comparables, prior transactions or a DCF.
- Take a look at the management team. Are there any red flags? Have they done a good job up until this point and is there any reason to believe they won't continue running the company well?
- The execution stage mostly just involves logging into an investment portal and placing a trade, however extra attention needs to paid if the security is thinly traded. Continuous monitoring of the security is part of the execution phase.

Conclusion

For those of us who weren't expecting to get into such depth in the pure investment capital phase, props for continuing to read through. There was a lot of wood to chop. At the end of the day, investing through a well-diversified and well-balanced portfolio can be accomplished in many ways—from simple index funds and ETFs to more complex research and investing strategies. It is up to the individual to decide which path best suits them, but hopefully some useful tools have become accessible after our discussion. Investing is fascinating, due to the infinite number of ways one can approach it, and with a solid foundation, a savvy investor should be well on his or her way toward making their capital work for them in the quest for financial independence.

The beauty of this system is that once it is in place, all that is required is periodic maintenance. We don't have to start from scratch all over again. And, as one reads and learns over time, they can improve their system, to further optimize performance.

Next, after Phase 3, we'll take a look at several important applications of the saving and investing concepts we've discussed: debt, housing, and taxes.

PART 2
SELECT APPLICATIONS

DEBT

Debt is one person's liability, but another person's asset.
Paul Krugman, *End This Depression Now!*

As I was writing this book, I quickly came to realize that the treatment of debt and borrowing in our financial lives really deserves its own section. If the path to financial freedom ends in a stress-free wallet experience, then debt is the troll hiding under the bridge. Never fear, we brought reinforcements.

Debt is tricky. On the one hand, the ability to borrow can be a powerful tool. In fact, many businesses use debt to their advantage, to increase returns on their investments,[36] bridge cash flow gaps (such as needing to finance up-front inventory before revenues are generated), and benefit from the tax deductibility of interest payments.

In addition, for the individual and when done correctly, borrowing by way of a mortgage to buy a house, or taking out loans to finance a college education, can be very additive to personal wealth. There may be government programs to help consumers borrow responsibly and achieve

---

[36] Borrowing can enhance company value if the return on investment is higher than the borrowing cost.

life goals that would otherwise be outside of their reach. With that in mind, it would be wrong to view debt as inherently negative.

But at some point, many people find themselves struggling to meet the interest and principal payments related to their past borrowings. Debt can cause significant stress, as the threat of bankruptcy or a heavily reduced budget (i.e., cutting costs to pay for debt service) looms like an insurmountable obstacle.

Debt—especially consumer debt—also has a way of creating a vicious cycle of high interest payments and reduced cash flow, which may necessitate the need for more debt just to pay for the old debt. This cycle can destroy personal finances like a tornado, making it hard for everyday consumers to get their lives back in order.

Given such positive and negative attributes, debt should be viewed in context. The attractiveness or unattractiveness of taking on debt has to do with the unique circumstances of the person doing the borrowing, as well as their "use of proceeds," or what they intend to spend that borrowed money on. Here, in our debt discussion, we focus on illustrating the different types of consumer debt out there and figuring out ways to reduce the burden of debt over time.

Mapping Out the Consumer Debt Landscape

There are many different kinds of debt, but we can make some broad classifications to try and understand the various types.

Secured Debt

Secured debt means that creditors (aka lenders) have recourse to a specific asset if a borrower fails to make interest or principal payments (i.e., if they default). This collateral helps the lender feel better about giving someone their money because they aren't just relying on a promise to be paid back. Recourse would allow the lender to apply to the courts in order to foreclose on the borrower's property, the seizure of which would be used to satisfy the obligation. Because of this foreclosure option, secured debt typically has a lower interest rate than its unsecured debt counterpart, in which lenders have no recourse to any of your specific assets. These are the most common types of secured debt:

Mortgage Debt

A mortgage contract is a debt taken out to finance a home purchase. Lenders such as a bank will typically finance 80% of a borrower's home purchase price, although higher LTV ("loan to value") ratios are available, under select circumstances. The 30-year, fully amortizing mortgage is the most common option, where borrowers make a monthly payment that satisfies both their interest and principal obligations over the life of the loan. At the end of the loan, the debt has been completely paid off (there is no final payment as there sometimes is with other forms of debt). If a borrower defaults, the bank can seize the house and try to sell it to recoup their loan.

Automobile loan

This is a debt undertaken in order to purchase a car. Again, auto loans are typically secured, so if borrowers fail to meet payments, the lender can repossess the car.

Leases

If someone doesn't want to buy a house or car, or can't afford the down payment yet, they can choose to rent by signing a lease. For our purposes, leasing is the same as taking on a debt because it allows someone to use an asset in exchange for promising to make periodic payments. The major difference is that at the end of a lease, the person leasing must return the asset. Companies that offer leases aren't typically nonprofits: They make money by renting out the use of their fleet of cars or residential properties. Leasing something can mean paying more over the life of the asset than would otherwise be the case if it had been purchased outright. After all, the leasing company has to earn a profit margin on its purchase and subsequent rental to you. All else being equal, their profit margin is an extra cost to you, the lessee.

Tax Liens

Failure to pay the taxes or fines on a specific asset, such as a house, car, boat, and so on, can prompt the government entity to which the taxes or fines are owed to place a lien on a specific asset. The most common example of this is having one's car impounded for unpaid parking tickets. Not fun.

Unsecured Debt

Sometimes, people borrow without assigning anything to secure their debt. That means the lender has no specific asset to seize if the loan is unpaid. This is a real "trust me, I'm good for it" situation. Because the lender has no foreclosure option on any specific assets, lenders see unsecured debt as riskier and typically charge a higher interest rate, to compensate for that. Common types of unsecured consumer debt include:

Credit Card Debt

This might be the biggest troll hiding under the bridge. Credit card debt has some of the highest interest rates on anything in the consumer debt landscape. Credit card purchases are often used to finance everyday items like groceries, fuel or various service expenses; sometimes, however, because they're easy to use, credit cards can tempt people to buy what they don't really need or can't afford. Many credit cards offer rewards to the cardholder in terms of points or cash back to incentivize spending. Cardholders may also receive an extended warranty on goods they purchase at no extra charge. As we'll see, the best way to use a credit card is to pay off the balance each month. That means, you'll be planning how you'll pay off the cost, before putting something on plastic. Recently, companies have been promoting Buy Now Pay Later as a payment option, which allows consumers to spread out the cost of their purchases over time, in a way similar to a credit card. While typically charging no interest, this option might be tempting. However, users should remember that it is still a form of debt—they are buying something with an obligation to pay it back later.

Student Loan Debt

Students nowadays often borrow funds to obtain some form of higher education. It doesn't have to be for an undergraduate or graduate college degree, but that is the most common use case. There are two primary types of student loan debt to keep in mind: (i) federal student loan debt, in which money is owed directly to the government and typically carries a subsidized (reduced) interest rate, and (ii) private student loan debt, which may come from a variety of sources (most of which are banks) and usually carries a higher interest rate.

Personal Loan

A personal loan is simply an unsecured loan from a bank or other financial institution (or even from a family member) that doesn't have recourse to any specific assets of yours. Terms may vary by the loan, for example providing tighter or looser restrictions on the use of the proceeds.

Medical Debt or Other Unpaid Bills

Unpaid medical or other bills are an obligation owed to the provider of the product or service that you consumed. Again, while these may not feel like debt, they are real obligations, nonetheless.

As can be seen even from this quick list, there are quite a few different flavors of debt. No wonder our mailboxes end up stuffed with advertisements from consumer lenders who are looking to "help." Let's take a look at some ways to reduce our debt burden.

Avoid Debt in the First Place

The easiest way to avoid excessive debt burdens is to avoid taking out debt in the first place. This is common sense, but it deserves a few sentences. Avoiding debt flows directly out of the sound budgeting practices discussed in Phase 2 as well as the long-term, goal-oriented planning illustrated throughout this book.

The main distinction to make in terms of what kinds of borrowing to avoid concerns the use of the proceeds. Money borrowed for purchases can either be spent on consumption or invested. As a rule, I feel that borrowing to fund consumption should be avoided because the benefit of the consumption disappears while the debt sticks around, while borrowing to fund investment might make sense depending on the context.

Consumption represents purchases of goods or services that give us a one-time benefit before disappearing. Investments, on the other hand, aren't used up, and we expect them to benefit us for multiple periods to come. In this case, I'm referring to any long-term asset that produces value as an investment. This could of course apply to financial assets such as stocks or bonds, but what we are mostly discussing in this section relates to non-financial assets like homes, cars, an education, etc. These are the things most often funded with consumer debt, which is our focus here.[37]

An example of the difference between consumption and investment is the difference between taking an Uber ride or buying a car. The benefits of buying an Uber ride end when you get dropped off, while the benefits of owning a car extend long after the initial purchase.

Borrowing to fund consumption usually comes in the form of an unsecured loan, which may seem like "free money" at the time, but that can come back to bite you hard, in the future. Psychologically, borrowing to fund consumption may seem like a good idea, because you get the benefit of whatever you are consuming up front, while the cost (in the form of interest, principal, and other non-cash costs) are borne out over

---

[37] What's more, borrowing to fund stock or bond investments can be especially tricky because of price changes in the underlying assets. It isn't something that is likely suitable.

multiple periods. However, this is a trap: it destroys wealth, due to interest payments and opportunity costs—which represent potential investments that were foregone to pay for the consumption.

Let's see how that works.

Consider Skylar, who is trying to decide when to take a $1,000 trip to Aruba (in truth, I've never been to Aruba but have heard it's great). Skylar doesn't have any savings at the moment (she must be contemplating this trip before reading this book), and so if she wants to go on the trip now she would have to fund it with her credit card. Let's say interest on her credit card runs 15% annually—roughly the U.S. average.[38] Also, let's say Skylar can save $100/month from her job going forward.

Funding the Aruba excursion with borrowing today would mean that Skylar will have to take out $1,000 of credit card debt at 15% interest. If she used all her savings each month to pay off debt ($100 per month), it would take her about 11 months to be debt-free. Putting a vacation on a credit card is a classic example of borrowing to fund consumption that could be dangerous. What's more, Skylar will have paid about $75 in interest, which is the cost of borrowing the money.

If instead, Skylar simply saved and invested her $100 each month, then by month 11 she would have accumulated $1,156 assuming a 12% annualized return on her investments. In this case, she could go on the trip for $1,000 and bank the remaining $156 in her savings.

Using credit card debt forces Skylar to pay an additional $75 in interest, but if she had waited and invested, she would have an extra $156 saved. That's a total swing of $231 ($75 + $156) or more than 20% of the cost of the trip. 20% is a lot! If this happened over 10 trips, that is more than $2,000 of lost wealth, never mind the amount that could eventually

---

[38] Federal Reserve: "Consumer Credit."

be saved had this $2,000 been invested. My bet is that by saving for the trip instead of splurging today, Skylar might find that she enjoys her time on the beaches of Aruba much more than she would have otherwise. Using the 11 months of downtime to figure out ways to reduce the vacation cost further, such as by booking a flight during an off-peak time, renting a cheaper accommodation, or using travel points, might make an even bigger impact on her budget.

It might sound like the implication from this example is to delay and reduce travel spending or that vacations are wasted money, but that is far from the point. The lesson here is more that borrowing for consumption purposes should be avoided, because it's a double whammy: you lose the money that you consumed, and you have to pay interest, on top of it, while you forsake potential investment returns. In fact, because of her sound money management, Skylar would be able to consume more in the future had she saved and invested. If she followed this template and ended up saving a few hundred dollars instead of spending $75 on interest for the Aruba trip, she would be able to save for her next vacation much quicker, or could take a larger or longer vacation next time. Her long-term consumption power rises faster than the waves on the shores of Aruba (or so I've heard—again, I've never been).

Borrowing to Fund an Investment

As alluded to, borrowing to fund investment might make sense—or not—depending on the context. The late great Marty Whitman, whom I was lucky enough to observe for several years at Third Avenue Management, puts this concept succinctly in his book, *Modern Security Analysis (2013).*

Three elements go into the determination of creditworthiness for functional purposes:

1. *Amount of debt*
2. *Terms of debt*
3. *How productive is the use of proceeds from incurring the debt?*

Of these, we argue that the third element is the most important.

The reference to "creditworthiness" means the amount of borrowing that a company or person has taken on relative to the amount and quality of assets they have.

In this section, I am referring to nonfinancial investments, so not the stocks, bonds, or other items that were covered in Phase 3. Here, we can think of nonfinancial investments as assets, from which we'll derive benefits more than once (i.e., everything that doesn't fall into the consumption category). The three main assets that people often borrow to buy include houses, cars, and higher education. In each case, some basic principles apply.

Perhaps the most critical question to answer when pondering a loan to finance an investment purchase is: Would this purchase make sense from an investment standpoint if we bought it using 100% cash? No borrowing. Then, we can ask: Will the use of debt enhance the benefits of making this purchase?

As to the first question, many of the same principles that we've discussed in Phases 2 and 3 apply to thinking about nonfinancial investments. Let's take a concrete example. If two houses are both available in the same neighborhood, were built at the same time with exactly the same materials on plots of land that are the same size, and if one house is priced at $1 million and the other at $750,000, a good investment decision would be to buy the cheaper house, because we get the most bang for our buck.

Likewise, if my earnings are expected to increase by $30k annually by getting a certain college degree and that degree costs me $100k, then it probably makes sense, all things being equal, to go for the degree. Phrased numerically, $30,000 of "reward" per $100,000 of cost is a 30% pretax yield on investment, quite attractive compared to alternative opportunities, such as stocks or bonds.[39]

Each of these examples stands on its own two feet in terms of investment merits, with or without the use of borrowing. This brings us to the second question: Does borrowing enhance the benefits of making this purchase? Most of the time, the reason for borrowing for nonfinancial investment purchases is a cash mismatch: We need the cash today to make the purchase, but the benefits are spread out over time. Borrowing helps bridge that gap, so we only have to come up with a 20% down payment on a house, for example (sometimes much less) or we can pay for college up front and then use our enhanced income to pay off the student loan debt. Funding a college degree or home purchase up front wouldn't be possible in most cases without the use of debt.

Note that for nonfinancial assets, it can be a little tricky to understand or quantify the monetary benefit side of the equation. For the higher education purchase, the monetary benefit is the increased earnings power available to someone with a certain degree. We will discuss the economics of owning a house in a subsequent chapter. For a car purchase, the monetary benefit is the savings from not having to pay for alternative modes of transportation (ride shares, public transport etc). In all cases,

---

[39] If, instead, we could only increase our earnings by $1k annually by purchasing the $100k degree, it probably doesn't make sense from an investment standpoint. We'd be earning a 1% return, which isn't attractive. Since it wouldn't make sense to do that with 100% cash, it definitely doesn't make sense to borrow to finance the degree.

there are nonmonetary side effects (other benefits or costs) that manifest themselves.

Numerically, a simple rule of thumb for evaluating the use of debt in investments is to compare the return on the investment with the cost of the debt. If the investment return is higher than the cost of the debt, then—at least mathematically—the use of debt will be beneficial (leaving riskiness aside for a second). For example, if an investment produces a 10% return and is financed with debt that only costs 5% in interest payments, this is a value-enhancing use of debt. We could invest $100, earn $10 of return, pay $5 of interest and be left with $5 for ourselves without having to put any of our own money down. Again, it is a little harder to quantify the returns of nonfinancial investments so precisely, but this is the financial concept that is going on in the background.

Here's the takeaway: don't use debt to finance consumption, and only use debt to finance investment purchases if those purchases would stand on their own two feet, without the use of said debt.

Pay Down Debt As A Form Of Investment

Last, let's look at the particular economics of paying down debt, in the context of a person with two or more debt obligations outstanding.

The financial cost of taking on debt is the periodic interest payments that are due. Interest payments are the price that lenders charge their clients to use the lender's money. It can be helpful to think of interest costs as a subscription fee that borrowers pay, in order to use someone else's money. Leaving debt outstanding longer than it has to be is akin to forgetting to cancel that Netflix subscription, even though you've already seen all the shows on the platform and accidentally broken your television.

Paying down debt is actually closely related to investing—so closely related, in fact, that we can consider them one and the same. To see why, let's use the example of Timothy, a xylophone technician with $1,000 in cash, $1,000 in debt outstanding and two options for using the cash:

- Option 1 is to pay down the $1,000 of a debt that carries a 5% interest rate.

- Option 2 is to keep the debt outstanding and invest $1,000, with an expected return of 5%.

Let's say Timothy chooses Option 2 (invest the money). Since he still has the $1,000 of debt outstanding, Timothy will owe the lender $50 at the end of the year ($1,000*5% interest), which is exactly equal to the expected $50 generated by the $1,000 investment: The cash generated from the investment can be used to pay down interest. Net cash flow in this case is 0, and net worth is also 0.

If Timothy chooses Option 1 and pays down the debt directly, he will get rid of the $50 interest obligation and be left with 0 net cash flow, just as he is in Option 1. Again, net worth is 0. We reach the same end result.

Cash	$ 1,000.0
Debt	$ (1,000.0)
Net Worth	$ -
Interest Rate on Debt	5.0%

Scenario 1: Pay Down Debt			Scenario 2: Keep Debt & Invest Cash		
Debt Outstanding	$	-	Debt Outstanding	$	(1,000)
Cash	$	-	Interest Paid During Year	$	(50)
Interest Paid During Year	$	-	Total Paid on Debt	$	(1,050)
Starting Net Worth	$	-	Investments Outstanding	$	1,000
Ending Net Worth	$	-	Profit on Investments	$	50
			Total Received on Investments	$	1,050
			Starting Net Worth	$	-
			Ending Net Worth	$	-

Figure 5.1: Paying down debt versus investing.

If Timothy left the debt outstanding and simply held the cash (Option 3?), then he'd owe $50 in interest on the debt but would have generated $0 from our cash—assuming no interest income on his cash balance. This is a loss of $50 in aggregate and not a great—or even a good—outcome.

Hence, assuming the interest rate on debt is the same as the expected return from investing the cash, we get to the same underlying cash flow and net worth whether we invest the extra cash or pay down debt directly. This is why we say that paying down debt is the same as investing at whatever interest rate the debt carries (in this case, 5%).

But this leads us to another interesting conclusion, because paying down debt is actually a risk-free investment, from our standpoint. That is, we are guaranteed to "earn" the interest rate on our debt by paying it down. This isn't true if we simply invest in stocks or bonds that entail risk. For example, on that investment mentioned above, Timothy could end up earning 3% instead of the 5% expected return, which wouldn't be enough to cover the interest costs on his debt.

This point is subtle but important. When we borrow money, most of the time lenders are going to charge us a higher interest rate than they themselves are borrowing at and will definitely charge us a higher interest rate than what is considered "risk free" in an economy, which is usually the rate at which the government borrows.[40] A private loan might require interest payments of more than 3 percentage points above the "risk-free" rate, to account for the higher probability that an individual borrower will default. This is called the interest rate "spread." If risk-free rates on 10-year government debt are 2% and our lender charges us 6%, we would say that the interest rate spread for us is 4%.

---

[40] For example the interest rate that the Treasury pays on a 10-year bond.

This positive spread is a relative disadvantage borne by the average consumer borrower. It is also the main force driving people to improve their credit scores; all else being equal, better credit scores mean lower spreads and lower borrowing costs.

However, what starts out as a disadvantage when we borrow—having to pay more in interest than the risk-free rate—flips around and turns into an advantage when we pay down debt. That is, when we pay down debt, we "earn" a return above the risk-free rate equal to whatever our interest rate is, but we take on no incremental risk ourselves. This is a powerful conclusion and the main reason why paying down debt should be viewed as an awesome investment. After all, savvy investors are always looking for ways to earn high returns with low risk, and paying down debt entails just that type of opportunity. To put some numbers around it, assume that the risk-free rates are 2%. Someone who pays down debt with a 7% interest rate has just found a way to invest their money risk-free at 7%, when all other participants in the market can only earn 2% on risk-free investments. Boo-yah.

As a result of that conclusion and when viewing debt paydown as an investment, it makes sense to pay down one's highest-cost debt first, because that is the highest return option available. Paying down 10% interest rate debt, instead of 5% interest rate debt, is akin to earning a 10% return rather than a 5% return, without taking any additional risk. That's a no-brainer for the smart personal capital allocator.

This certainly doesn't mean that taking on debt is beneficial on its own, just because the opportunity to pay it down later is an attractive investment opportunity. Rather, for someone who already has debt outstanding, using an investment lens is merely the strategic rationale for paying down high-cost debt first.

Debt Paydown in the Context of Our Capital Allocation Framework

At this point, many readers may be wondering about how this idea of debt paydown as an investment corresponds to our overall views of capital allocation, as I've laid them out in Part 1. In other words, how do we decide when to pay down debt and when to invest directly, instead? Assuming the broader stock market continues to deliver annual returns in the 8% to 10% range, as it has historically, wouldn't it make sense never to pay down debt and, instead, to always keep as much money as possible in the market?

I have a few thoughts on these questions. First, the higher the interest rate on our debt, relative to our expected returns in the market, the more our focus should shift to debt paydown, because as we've mentioned, the debt paydown is essentially risk-free. In this way, those with credit card debt or high-interest student loan debt have a relatively easy decision: Their interest rates are often in the 6% to 10% range, if not higher for many credit card relationships. Between a risk-free investment of paying down debt in the 6% to 10% interest rate range or investing for the long term in the market at 8% to 10% prospective returns, I think the low-stress option is usually going to be debt paydown. Note that stress levels and the goal of reducing stress are among the key positive side effects of debt paydown. If we were able to quantify these benefits, one might conclude that debt paydown is actually better than a risk-free investment because of these enhancements to one's quality of life!

So, the higher the interest rate on our debt relative to what we think we can earn in the market, the more likely we should be to use incoming savings to pay the debt down, all else being equal.

On the other hand, if we have particularly low-cost debt outstanding, such as a mortgage secured against our house that carries a low interest rate of, say, 3.5%, then rather than accelerating the mortgage paydown, we might feel comfortable investing for the long-term in the market and earning 8% to 10% returns.

However, we have to consider the probability of earning that expected 8% to 10% in the market. This ties back to our discussions of risk in Phase 3. How likely is it that we will be able to achieve those returns? As part of Phase 3, we built out an infrastructure using our waterfall mechanism and employing the Three Heroes of Capital Allocation. As you may remember, the second "Hero" is the Flex account, which is a bucket of money that holds our emergency funds as well as a war chest to be used for opportunistic investments. The war chest may increase or decrease, depending on how many attractive opportunities there are in the market. Depending on how hot the market is, we can flex that war chest up or down to buy when others are scared and to sell when others are exuberant.

We can use the war chest analogy in thinking about how to allocate dollars between investing and additional debt paydown once we've paid down high-cost debt. When the market is on a tear, we could try to shift our focus to debt paydown, because as the market rises, the probability of earning that 8% to 10% average market return goes down. With a lower probability of earning a good return, we might be better off doing the sure thing of paying down debt. This may seem a bit wishy-washy: are all of those reading this now supposed to analyze the entire stock market, to find out if it is over- or undervalued? As usual, the brilliant Howard Marks has something noteworthy to say on this point:

> We may never know where we are going, but we better have a good idea where we are … and act accordingly.
>
> Howard Marks, *The Most Important Thing*

What I take away from this quote is that even though investors can't predict the future (which they can't), they should be able to get a pretty good sense of whether the market is a little too hot or a little too cold. Hot markets tend to have similar characteristics: a surge in prices over and above fundamental cash flow growth (for example, causing the S&P 500 price/earnings ratio to increase, something that a quick Google search will show), a deluge of initial public offerings, the emergence of speculators and day traders who are trying to get rich quickly off of the ride, an increase in headlines about the stock market where such headlines seldomly appear, etc. One "sanity check" that I've found helpful is to look at *The Wall Street Journal*'s list of new 52-week highs and new 52-week lows. These lists show the companies that are at their highest or lowest point in the past year, respectively. When the market is hot, there are tons of companies on the 52-week high list and very few companies on the 52-week low list. Vice versa when investors are pessimistic.

Whichever way one goes about trying to gauge the heat of the market, the point isn't to overmanage your portfolio or to stress out trying to time investments; but a general sense of how things sit is helpful both in allocating money from the war chest in our Flex Capital account and in deciding whether to use that surplus dollar of savings to pay down debt or invest in the market. As much art as science.

Should We Try a Piece of the Refi Pie?

As a close cousin of direct debt paydown, refinancing involves taking out an entirely new loan to satisfy an existing loan. Understanding when an option to refinance makes sense boils down to a basic cost/benefit analysis. The benefit of refinancing is typically a lower interest rate, longer time to maturity or otherwise more flexible loan terms. Refinancing may come with a monetary cost, however, in the form of closing fees or costs to extinguish the old loan. It's important to compare the savings from lower interest rates to the costs to refinance the loan. Since extending the time to maturity may not result in monetary savings, we are focusing on reducing the interest rate, as our primary objective.

If a lower interest rate is going to save us $2,000/year on our 10-year loan, and it costs us $4,000 to refinance, then it probably makes sense to do so because of the payback period, which is how long it takes those savings to cover our costs. In this case, the payback period is 2 years on the 10-year loan, calculated as the $4,000 in refi costs, divided by the $2,000 we save each year ($4,000/$2,000 = 2). If the same $2,000/year savings were available on a 3-year loan, however, and it cost us $7,000 to refinance, then it wouldn't be in our best interest to do so: In this case, the payback period would exceed the lifetime of the loan. This is shown by dividing the $7,000 refi costs by the $2,000 annual savings, and $7,000/$2,000 = 3.5 years. So, we wouldn't have enough time to earn back the investment in refinancing costs.

To summarize, one of the keys to personal financial freedom is to understand debt and how to make debt work in your favor as a tool, rather than against you as a sinkhole. Sinkholes are lame.

Toolkit Summary—Debt Reduction

- Debt isn't inherently good or bad. It is more about what the terms of the debt are, and what we do with the proceeds.

- There are many kinds of debt. Some are secured—meaning the lender can take a specific asset if the loan isn't repaid—and some aren't. Unsecured debts usually have higher interest rates.

- As a rule, try not to borrow to fund consumption. Borrowing to fund an investment—such as an education or home purchase—could be a good idea but it depends on the merit of the investment relative to the cost of the debt.

- Paying down debt works the same as investing. Actually, debt-paydown is quite a good investment because it is virtually risk-free.

- Refinancing could be a good option depending on the reduction in interest costs relative to the cost of refinancing.

HOUSING

It's always a dream house until you realize you don't want all the things you dreamed. Why am I doing this? I just want a closet and a gym.
Venus Williams, interview, *The Washington Post*

The utilization of shelter is one of the key things separating us from our nomadic, hunter-gatherer ancestors. Combined with agricultural breakthroughs, the ability to occupy a permanent residence was one of the primary reasons civilizations could form and prosper. The elimination of a nomadic day-to-day freed up an awful lot of time for the citizens, which they promptly filled with thinking about housing—and for good reason.

Renting, buying, building, owning, fixing, investing in, or selling a residence takes a lot of work. Meanwhile, a home is typically the largest single asset that a person owns outside of their retirement portfolio—and a mortgage is likely to be the largest debt outstanding. Housing expenditures usually eat up the lion's share of the household budget. What's more, many people decide to invest in residential rental properties to build wealth. Those four walls really matter for financial outcomes. It is fitting, then, that the second applied topic we will discuss is housing. Understanding the numbers is well worth the effort.

I've spent a bit of time on housing already in this book, primarily by way of Phase 2 in which we looked at a few methods for cutting housing costs. In this section, we will take a broader view of housing affordability and unpack the theory behind these expenses, paying particular attention to the question of renting vs. buying. Then, we look at some alternatives to traditional homeownership that could come in handy.

In Chapter 4: Debt Reduction, we discuss the difference between investment and consumption expenditures and find that consumption expenditures are used up in a short period of time and aren't expected to produce any benefits beyond their initial use. Investment expenditures, on the other hand, can be expected to produce benefits for multiple periods— usually measured in years—from now.

The difference between consumption and investment is a very useful thing to keep in mind when evaluating financial decisions generally. It is critical to our understanding of housing affordability, as well. Investments in housing are key to building long-term wealth because housing costs are so large relative to the rest of our expenses. The way we apply the concept in this section is to categorize our expenditures for housing as either consumption or investment. Investment expenditures lead directly to more equity in our homes, which is the end goal of building wealth through housing. Then, we compare those expenditures to our income or earnings potential, to develop a clearer view of the affordability of different housing options.

Consumption vs. Investment Expenditures for Housing

Most renters pay one monthly bill to their landlord, which covers the right to use their apartment under a lease agreement (door-to-window water slides are typically prohibited in these agreements, so don't get any ideas). They are also likely to pay for at least some utilities (heat and hot water may be included in the rent, while electricity and a broadband connection may not; situations vary). Renter's insurance is an additional cost.

In all cases (rent, utilities and insurance), the payment made covers the period for which the service is being used, with no obligation from either party after the period ends. For example, we don't expect to make any payments to our electricity provider after we are out of the apartment. In that regard, these expenses are "consumed" in the current month, and we settle up fully with the service provider for what we used. For renters, the distinction between consumption and investment is simple: Pretty much everything is consumption. Money flows from the renter to the landlord and other service providers, and that's that.

For homeowners, the situation is a bit more complicated, which is why pinning down the attractiveness of buying a house takes some thinking. In most cases, homeowner's expenses are composed of interest and principal payments on a mortgage, property taxes, homeowner's insurance, utilities, repair and maintenance, larger home improvement projects, and other miscellaneous expenses.

In terms of what would be classified as consumption, the interest payments, property taxes, insurance, utilities and basic periodic repairs are consumed in the period for which they are paid. These costs aren't expected to increase our equity or add value to the home in future periods, and so shouldn't be considered investment. You can pay mortgage interest, or a heating bill, all day long, but it won't make you wealthy. Two expense items, however—principal payments and larger home improvement projects—can be expected to increase our equity in future periods and so can be looked at as investment.

Assuming there has been no change to the underlying home value, paying down the principal balance of a mortgage increases our equity in the home, dollar for dollar. If the bank owns less of our home, we own more. And, as we saw in Chapter 4, paying down principal has the equivalent effect on our finances as investing that capital and earning a return equal to the interest rate on the debt. Hence, principal payments can be thought of as an investment expenditure, with the pre-tax return on that investment equal to the interest rate on the debt. Paying down principal on a 4.5% mortgage would be like investing and earning a 4.5% return, a concept straight out of Chapter 4.[41]

Likewise, larger projects that add value to the home, such as installing a generator, putting in new cabinets, paving the driveway, replacing the roof, etc., are expected to produce benefits for multiple years to come and may increase the home value by more than the cost of doing the project. For example, if it is a desirable feature, a $10,000 generator installation project may increase one's home value by, say $15,000. Investing $10,000 and winding up with a home worth an additional $15,000 seems like a great investment, but it isn't always the case that home improvement projects make smart economic sense. Whether or not a project is a smart investment depends on the value produced by the project relative to its cost. If that new generator only increased the home value by $5,000 then it technically wouldn't be worth the $10,000 cost. That said, other nonfinancial benefits, such as peace of mind during a thunderstorm, should clearly be considered.

---

[41] Note that this refers to pre-tax returns. Paying down principal would mean that the homeowner loses the ability to deduct the associated interest on their taxes, so the actual impact on their overall cash flow after taxes would be less than just the 4.5% return would imply. We will get into the intersection of taxes and real estate in the next section. The 4.5% return on an investment may or may not involve a tax liability in the year it is made.

The goal of classifying these expenditures is to understand what money is truly leaving every period and then to use that analysis to figure out what housing options are affordable and whether owning vs. renting makes sense. In the owning vs. renting conversation, we should compare the total cost to renters (rent, utilities, and insurance) to the consumption expenditures for homeowners (interest, insurance, property tax, and routine maintenance). To make the comparison consistent, principal and large home improvement projects shouldn't be factored in.

Let's say Maria, from Part 1, rents an apartment. She pays $2,300 in rent, $100 in utilities and $10 in renter's insurance each month, making her total monthly consumption of housing costs $2,410 ($2,400 + $100 + $10). If Maria could buy a house and arrange a monthly mortgage payment of $2,500, slightly higher utilities of $150/month, property taxes of $300/month, and insurance of $100/month, her total payment would be $3,050 ($2,500 + $150 + $300 + $100). However, of her $2,500 monthly mortgage payment, she'd be paying roughly $750 in principal at the outset of the loan (assuming a 4.0% interest rate on the 30-year mortgage). This $750 is an investment, because it reduces Maria's debt and contributes directly to her equity. Hence, we should strip this out of her total payments to arrive at a true "consumption" expenditure of $2,300 (=$3,050 - $750). From this perspective, she is actually saving $110 vs. renting ($2,300 ownership cost vs. her $2,410 cost to rent), without even considering the tax impact of deducting her interest payments, or the potential for home price appreciation over time—each of which is important. As time goes on, Maria will be paying down more and more principal each period—and reducing her interest expense—which means even more of her total monthly payment could be classified as investment.

There are several ways to analyze housing affordability once we understand the differences between consumption and investment.

Readers may find it helpful to compute income coverage, which is the proportion of income eaten up by housing costs. Again, breaking this out by consumption and investment expenses can provide a more realistic sense of the true economic cost of housing. High ratios of rent or ownership costs relative to income is a warning sign. One heuristic I've seen is that housing costs shouldn't take up more than a third of one's pretax income, so if Maria earns $60,000 per year she should aim to spend no more than $20,000 per year (or around $1,700 per month) on housing. This applies to total costs, including investment expenditures like principal paydown. The goal of thinking about income coverage is making sure that we have enough cash coming in each month to pay our housing costs and still have enough left over for other expenses, saving, and investing. If we own a home, we might be more comfortable with a higher ratio because some of that payment is investment spending. Both art and science are involved.

Home price ratios are another useful metric, and compare the total cost of a home relative to one's income. This is similar to a price/earnings ratio for a stock. In most areas of the U.S., home prices range between three to six-times one's annual income. In Maria's case, this would mean she could afford a home that costs between $180,000 and $360,000 (three to six times her pretax income).

Rent vs. own comparisons like the example above can help one decide if now is the right time to try and transition to homeownership. Housing market analysis is also a worthwhile pursuit. Are home prices rapidly rising, or have they been stable for a while? Are bidding wars and buyers waiving home inspections becoming more common, signifying a frothy market? Utilizing the investor instincts we've developed throughout this book—particularly in Phase 3—will come in handy here.

In the long term, homeowners have a few key advantages over renters that stem largely from the investment characteristics of buying. First, the consumption piece of the mortgage payment is actually falling over time. In most cases, total mortgage payments—the sum of interest and principal—are fixed. A fixed-rate mortgage that requires a $3,000 monthly payment in year two will also require a $3,000 monthly payment in year 20. During this time, interest costs decline because principal is paid down—this is known as amortization.

What's more, property taxes should be correlated with home values, so that in essence, any increase in these taxes is being "paid for" by a higher home value, and increased home equity. If the local municipality realizes my home is worth $100,000 more and I owe $1,000 of additional property taxes because of that, then I still come out quite positively—although the property taxes are paid in cash and I won't benefit from the home price appreciation until I sell. Insurance and utility costs can be expected to be relatively stable for the homeowner. Repair and maintenance costs can be kept in check if our homeowner makes an effort to learn some handy skills and maintain the basic home systems.

Rent, however, may not be stable and probably won't be expected to decline the way that interest costs do for a homeowner. Renters are reliant on a friendly landlord to keep the rent at a stable level, which may or not be the case once it comes time to renew. Over longer periods of time, the average rent paid is very likely to go up, rather than down. In this way, the financial experience of renters versus homeowners in terms of their annual consumption expenditures may diverge quite materially as time progresses, in favor of the homeowner.

Homeowners do have to cope with the added up-front costs of a broker's fee (which may or may not apply to renters) and legal, title, and other closing expenses, as well as the maintenance costs which are typically handled by a landlord when renting.[42] For that reason, homeowners should try to maintain their ownership for at least three to five years after purchase, so as not to have to repeat these costs too frequently.

A simplified graphical depiction of total consumption costs for homeownership vs. renting might look something like this:

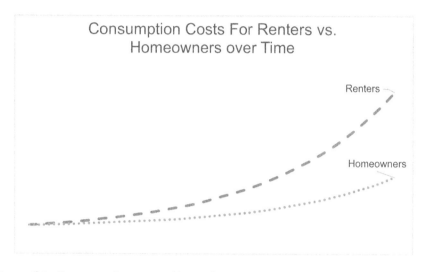

Figure 6.1: Consumption expenditures for owning versus renting, over time.

Notice how the gap between the two options grows as time progresses. While renters see an increase on their entire expense base each year, homeowners only see increases on expenses like property tax, maintenance, and insurance, while the interest costs on their mortgage actually decline as principal is paid down, which is why the line has a much shallower slope than that of the renters. Again, this doesn't factor in investment expenditures like principal paydown, and doesn't account for home price

[42] The broker's fee on a home purchase is likely to actually be paid by the seller, however if someone is buying a new home and selling their current home, they would have to pay a broker's fee as part of the total transaction. Further, broker's fees paid by sellers have the effect of raising prices in the market overall, which flows out of the buyer's wallet indirectly.

appreciation, but I think it is helpful directionally to show some of the benefits of owning over the long term due to the declining nature of interest expenses over the life of a mortgage.[43]

The second advantage for homeowners is the potential for home price appreciation, which renters don't benefit from. As the saying goes, they aren't making any more land (barring any large underwater biodome communities that may be found on your local sci fi channel). So, if buyers are careful not to rush into a market that is too hot—and overpay, as a result—then they can feel reasonably comfortable that over the long term, their home will increase in value, and their equity along with it. Renting, on the other hand, means that higher residential prices will accrue to the benefit of the landlord.

The third relative advantage that homeowners have over renters is the tax-deductibility of interest payments on their mortgage. Homeowners can use their interest payments to reduce taxable income, thereby lowering their tax bill. Renters have no such deductibility and are stuck paying their full rental obligation, in addition to the full tax bill on their income.

Overall, an investment in housing can provide real financial advantages over time. It is a key piece in the puzzle for achieving financial freedom. Setting aside some money each month strictly earmarked for a down payment on a house is a great way to make the transition to homeownership. Utilizing Phases 1 and 2 of this book to help get the personal cash flow in order could go a long way toward funding that savings effort.

---

[43] If we were to include home price appreciation and the tax benefits from mortgage interest deduction, the gap between owning and renting would appear even wider.

Strategies to Reduce Housing Costs

In Phase 2, we looked at some strategies to cut down on housing costs, so I won't repeat all of those here, but as usual the main thing is to be flexible and think entrepreneurially. Doing the work of researching markets and finding undervalued homes or apartments up front can save a lot of money down the line. It is an opportunity to be savvy about the search process and lock in a favorable residence. Approaching a new living situation as an investment opportunity can be a helpful mindset to adopt.

After moving in, one key strategy is to try and focus on how to monetize underutilized space. This could mean renting out an extra bedroom, storing a friend's extra personal belongings for a monthly payment (turning one's home into a small self-storage facility), or listing the apartment on Airbnb for a weekend when you are otherwise going to be out of town—assuming you comply with all local laws and regulations, in doing so. Installing solar panels or making other energy efficiency investments might take a helpful chunk out of monthly utility bills. Heck, if it is legal in the state you are operating in, maybe even turn that empty closet into a small-scale cannabis growing facility or refashion the corner grass into a chicken coop. It never hurts to think creatively about better monetizing one's real estate.

These little entrepreneurial adventures might help string together a permanent reduction in housing costs, with the savings allocated towards transitioning to homeownership or, if already a homeowner, investing in some new business ideas.

Alternatives to Traditional Homeownership

As indicated earlier, owning a home vs. renting one's residence has tangible long-term benefits that shouldn't be underestimated. Someone who can buy a residence and, over time, pay off the mortgage will most of the time get closer to financial freedom than someone who is a permanent renter. A lot of this has to do with the cost of carrying a home—those consumption expenditures—that either decline or increase at a rate much slower than average rent does, while investment expenditures (principal payments and larger home improvement projects) provide lasting benefits that can pay off in a big way if home price appreciation is strong or if the value created from the projects is high.

That said, owning one's primary residence isn't necessarily required, to achieve financial independence. Those of us who place a premium on the flexibility of renting might be interested in some of the investment strategies that follow.

Own Someone Else's Home Instead

It might seem a little far-fetched for someone to consider buying an investment property before they buy their own primary residence. Even so, there are a few benefits to consider. Outside of some legal and other costs to get the home ready for renters to occupy, the up-front expenditure should be basically the same as if you were going to live there . In addition, the consumption costs for a rental home actually look a lot better on an after-tax basis than owning a primary residence does, because landlords (owners of investment real estate) are able to deduct something called "depreciation" from their taxable income.

In this context, depreciation is a non-cash expense that landlords can deduct from the rental profits they earn. It is a feature of how the IRS treats property investing. These deductions lower one's tax liability even though they are non-cash expenses, sort of like having a coupon. This is one of the hidden gems of private real estate investing and is discussed further in the Tax chapter.

Finally, most rental properties can produce cash flow over and above the carrying costs of owning the home. That extra profit can be thought of as a reduction in one's own housing costs. For example, let's say Maria owns two identical houses, each with a total cost of $2,500 per month. If she rents one of them out for $3,000 per month and lives in the other, she will be paying down the mortgage on that investment property AND will have effectively reduced her own living costs by the extra profit (in this case, $500/month). This lowers the carrying costs on the home she lives in to $2,000 ($2,500 - $500). If Maria owns an investment property but lives in a rental instead, this is like getting a $500/month reduction in her rent while the tenant in her investment property pays down the mortgage and builds equity for her. At this point in the book, readers are starting to wonder if Maria is the next Warren Buffett. She might be.

Rent Your Primary Residence, Invest in Public Real Estate Securities

Owning someone else's home may be a great option, but not everyone wants to be a landlord. Plus, affording the down payment and other up-front costs for a rental property may be a tough hill to climb. Another way to generate some of the same benefits would be to "build equity in one's home" by investing what normally would go towards a down payment in public real estate securities, instead. Let me explain.

The returns for homeowners and landlords come primarily from home price appreciation, the tax deductibility of certain costs, the potential to improve the home through high-return projects, and, in the case of the landlord, rental income from tenants over and above the carrying costs of the property. The largest driver of returns will probably be home price appreciation and rental income. These factors generally move up and down with the broader real estate markets over time; in other words, the returns on our own private real estate investments tend to be at least loosely correlated to the real estate industry as a whole.

A savvy capital allocator could replicate these returns on their own, by taking funds they would have used for a down payment and investing them in public real estate securities, instead. Real estate investment trusts (REITs), homebuilders, mutual funds and ETFs invested in real estate should provide similar returns over time as being a landlord, and the entry price (the "down payment") is as small as the cost of buying a few shares. What's more, no property management skills on the part of the investor are required.

In fact, there are even REITs operating today that buy and operate large pools of single-family rental homes (search "Single Family Rental REITs"). A security like this should give the investor a return that is pretty close to the economics of home ownership outright or owning rental property.

This strategy could be a great intermediate step for someone who wants to benefit from the long-term advantages of home ownership, but who isn't yet ready to afford a down payment, or for someone who prefers a more hands-off approach to real estate investment.

Conclusion

All too often, housing costs occupy the nexus of financial stressors. Understanding the breakdown of housing expenditures into consumption and investment is a great start to forming a strategy for optimizing the wealth-creating potential of homeownership.

The ability to lower costs creatively by having an investor mindset about locating a desirable house or rental property and then monetizing excess space, pursuing high-return projects, and benefitting from home price appreciation should allow us to occupy more solid ground and get the real estate working for us, not the other way around.

Finally, owning a primary residence isn't the only option, especially for those craving more flexibility out of their residence. Transferring that down payment into an investment property or a basket of publicly traded real estate securities is a potentially valuable option to explore.

Toolkit Summary—Housing Affordability

- Understanding consumption vs. investment is an important part of analyzing housing affordability. Consumption is used up in the period it is paid for, while investments have long-lasting benefits.

- Housing costs that are consumed include all costs of renting. For homeowners, consumption might include interest payments, property taxes, insurance, utilities, and maintenance.

- Principal payments and larger home improvement projects can be thought of as investments because they produce benefits lasting longer than one year and add to the value of one's home equity.

- For a fair comparison between owning and renting, one should try to strip out the investment expenses of owning a home.

- Income coverage, home price ratios, rent vs. own comparisons and market analysis all help one develop a view on the attractiveness of different housing options.

- Two key advantages of homeownership are the potential for home price appreciation, and interest payments that go down as principal is paid off. The tax-deductibility of interest is a third.

- Strategies to lower housing costs could involve renting out excess space, turning the home into an Airbnb for a few weekends of the year, or other creative endeavors.

- There are ways to profit from home ownership without actually owning the home you live in. Owning a rental property (someone else's home) or investing in public real estate securities (REITs and other real estate stocks) are two areas to consider.

TAXES

A person doesn't know how much he has to be thankful for until he has to pay taxes on it.

Ann Landers

Quick question: What do buying an ice cream cone, receiving a paycheck, cashing out an investment winner, selling an investment loser, and living in your current home or apartment have in common? Yes, you guessed it: tax implications! Taxes are an inescapable (trust me, many have tried) reality of our civilization. While they are necessary to maintain law and order, fund the shared infrastructure we utilize, and provide a safety net for our least fortunate, the fact is that very few people enjoy paying their taxes.

Taxes feel like a cost, rather than an investment in our country. In many cases, particularly when inefficient or low-return government spending is involved, this view is justified. In many others, it is not. But hem and haw all we want, taxes need to be understood and dealt with intelligently by our savvy personal capital allocators. And what better place to deal with the topic of taxes than in the final chapter of *Working Capital*, after we've journeyed through the methods and strategies for saving and investing our money? After all, the pages in this book are geared toward generating more cash flow and profitability year in and year out, which inevitably will result in higher tax bills.

Our goal shouldn't be to do away with all tax payments (to which there is an easy answer: Move to Antarctica). That said, being efficient and optimal about the taxes we pay is a highly important component of generating and maintaining long-term wealth.

A quick author note: Michael Elias, CPA, contributed the "A Word From Michael" sections for this chapter and also provided guidance on the overall content. Michael is a licensed CPA and private tax consultant based in Detroit. He is also my cousin and has been a great mentor to me in regard to business, investing, and life since I was in middle school. Please give him a warm welcome!

Why Does Taxation Exist?

Just as companies rely on collective organizational hierarchies to survive,[44] so do civilizations rely on collective government and shared public resources to flourish. Driving to work on the highway, going to public school, and wondering why foreign invaders don't land on the shores of Connecticut more often are all governmental outcomes that have been funded by something, and that something is taxes. It is an "everybody pitch in" situation. Businesses have revenue; governments have taxes.

In fact, if governments were analyzed through the lens of a private business, they would rank at the top. They are monopolies, have pricing power, benefit from few substitutes, and have a favorable regulatory backdrop, to say the least. If only there was a way to invest in the government!

In Phase 3, we discussed municipal and federal government bonds as investments issued by governments. These securities typically have low

---

[44] Org. charts, divisions of labor, chains of command, standardized processes, etc.

interest rates, reflecting their perceived safety, which makes sense given how attractive this "government business model" is. Paying taxes is another form of investment in the government, although it isn't always seen this way.

Taxes Are An Investment in the Government

Tongue-in-cheek though it may be, I think this concept of taxes representing an investment in the government is actually a helpful one to have in mind. After all, many people pay tens of thousands of dollars per year in taxes, which means taxes are likely one of the largest expenditures in a household. If we were collectively putting that money into an investment account instead, the balance increase each year would be staggering (and most certainly enough to retire at a relatively young age). For example, $20,000 in taxes paid each year, compounded at a 10% annual return, would result in a >$3 million portfolio by the end of 30 years.

Figuring out whether this tax investment earns an attractive return and has an attractive risk profile is no different from the thought process we would use to analyze a business. How much do we have to put up, what is the risk, and what do we get out of it? In this case, most people have to "put up" something that looks like about a third of their income, 5% to 10% of the value of their purchases, 1% of the value of their home, and a quarter of their long-term investment gains, although variations in tax rates are the norm at the state and city level. What they receive in return are security, law and order, infrastructure, education, healthcare, and more, although the quality and quantity of those benefits can vary and be unpredictable. Many of these benefits—such as a new road—are long-term in nature. They aren't consumed in the period for which they are paid, which ties into our discussion of investment and consumption in the

Housing chapter. Maybe it doesn't make the most sense that people complain about paying their taxes but brag about their stock portfolio.

The tangential implication here is that tax efficiency is really important to long-term wealth creation because taxes represent such a large chunk of our spending, and the opportunity cost of paying excessive amounts of taxes can really crimp our ability to invest in attractive situations. Yes, we have to see Uncle Sam, and yes sometimes he hits the game-winner in pickup basketball, but do we have to be best friends?

Taxes Are an Incentive System

In addition to being the primary method—alongside borrowing—that governments use to fund their expenditures, taxes also represent a relatively efficient system for incentivizing different kinds of activity. Ever notice how cigarettes are taxed quite heavily, but many groceries aren't taxed at all? This is the government's way of getting people to favor buying fresh food over smoking. Or, how the interest on a mortgage is tax-deductible, but the rent expense on an apartment isn't? Purposeful or not, the taxes that governments put in place can really move the needle on influencing behavior.

In 1696, England instituted a tax on the number of windows a house had. The more windows, the more tax the building owner had to pay. Rather than actually pay this ludicrous tax, homeowners instead covered up their windows with bricks or wood. Fine, but this led to health problems down the line due to the reduction in clean air and light. The tax was repealed a short 156 years later. To summarize this bizarre period in tax history: The government spied a window of opportunity, the citizens quickly threw shade on the tax by bricking their windows, until finally the government was forced to shutter the idea. (Yes, pun intended.) Incentives matter.

There Are a Lot of Different Kinds of Taxes

Tax is a broad term that describes how governments collect money from their citizens (including commercial entities). But there are many different flavors of taxation that one should be aware of. The classifications I have found most useful for understanding taxes are jurisdiction and method.

Tax jurisdiction refers to the actual domain in which citizens are paying taxes. For most people, the jurisdictions they need to be aware of are municipal—city or town—state and federal. These correspond to the different government entities that need to collect taxes. Each government entity has its own set of funding requirements and budget, for which it attempts to set tax rates accordingly.

Taxes for municipal and state governments are easy to visualize because they relate to things we use every day as part of living in our current location. Roads, bridges, hospitals, emergency services, schools, etc. all rely on locally funded taxes. On the other hand, federal taxes are often used to fund broader programs and agencies such as the military, national healthcare programs, our federal court system, Congress, and social security. Federal tax dollars may also make their way to state or local governments as well, so these systems aren't mutually exclusive. Understanding the needs of the different government entities that call on us to fund them is one lens through which to understand the impact of our tax payments.

A second classification system for taxes relates to the method by which tax dollars are collected. The two primary methods are (1) income and expenditures, and (2) assets.

On the income side, we have regular income tax, which requires us to send the government a portion of our earnings. This income may derive itself from a few sources, such as a salary from a job, a bonus payment, receiving an inheritance (depending on the state you live in), or earning income from an investment. Investment income may be from dividends or interest income on a security we own or from the profits we receive from selling a security at a gain.

This last event is called a capital gain because we experienced a gain on the capital we invested (party lights and disco music, please). Capital gains can be further divided into short-term—a capital gain from one year or less—and long-term—for an investment gain earned over the course of multiple years. The key thing to remember with income taxes is that any time we receive a flow of cash for something we did, there is a high likelihood that the government will want a cut.

Note that income taxes in the U.S. operate in what's known as a progressive system. The progression is what people refer to when they talk about tax brackets. The more one makes, the higher tax bracket their marginal earnings go into. This doesn't mean that all of one's taxable income is taxed at the higher rate, just that the marginal—or "next"—dollars are. The tax brackets for 2022 are shown below.

2022 Tax Brackets				
TAX RATE	**Single**	**Head of Household**	**Married Filing Jointly or Qualifying widow(er)**	**Married Filing Separately**
10%	$0 to $10,275	$0 to $14,650	$0 to $20,550	$0 to $10,275
12%	$10,276 to $41,775	$14,651 to $55,900	$20,551 to $83,550	$10,276 to $41,775
22%	$41,776 to $89,075	$55,901 to $89,050	$83,551 to $178,150	$41,776 to $89,075
24%	$89,076 to $170,050	$89,051 to $170,050	$178,151 to $340,100	$89,076 to $170,050
32%	$170,051 to $215,950	$170,051 to $215,950	$340,101 to $431,900	$170,051 to $215,950
35%	$215,951 to $539,900	$215,951 to $539,900	$431,901 to $657,850	$215,951 to $323,925
37%	$539,901 to -	$539,901 to -	$657,851 to -	$323,926 to -

Figure 7.1 U.S. 2022 tax brackets.

Source: Internal Revenue Service

The way this works is fairly simple. Each tax bracket corresponds to a certain level of taxable income. For example, a single person with a taxable income of $50,000 would pay 10% on their first $10,275 of taxable income (or $1,027.5), then 12% on the next $31,479 of income between $10,276 and $41,775 (or $3,777.5, which is $31,479*12%), and finally 22% on the remaining $8,225 ($50,000 total income minus $41,775), which equals $1,809. The total amount of taxes due would therefore be $6,614. Note this only corresponds to federal taxes and doesn't include any state or city taxes that may also be due.

Expense-based taxes are generated when we spend money on things. Sales tax is the prime example here, and one reason many people drive to New Hampshire—where sales tax is nil—to load up on high-value goods. A luxury tax, which is a tax levied on nonessential or especially high-value goods, is another form of expense-based tax. Excise taxes on specific goods or services such as cigarettes and alcohol are other examples of expense-based taxes.

While income and expense-based taxes relate to taxes on flows of money coming in or out, asset-based taxes are levied on a store of wealth. Property taxes are the primary asset-based tax that consumers face. Most property taxes relate to real estate or cars. Property taxes are one of the primary ways that municipalities generate cash flow.

The actual tax rates on this flora and fauna of cash flows and assets are constantly changing and are heavily influenced by the spending proclivities of the powers at be. We can utilize this understanding of how taxes are collected to generate strategies for making efficient use of our tax dollars.

Deductions and Credits

Among the many aspects of paying our taxes, deductions and credits rank near the top of the list in terms of importance. Deductions, as the name implies, are expenses that we can subtract from our income to lower our tax bills. Larger deductions mean that our taxable income goes down. If Skylar has a $70,000 income but can deduct mortgage interest, property taxes, a home office, and some charitable donations that add up to $15,000, then she will have lowered her taxable income to $55,000 ($70,000 income - $15,000 of deductions). This $55,000 is what she will then pay taxes on, so she has cut her tax liability considerably.

Deductions in the U.S. have one important nuance to them, which is that everyone, no matter their expenses in a particular year, is eligible to take what's called the standard deduction. Taking the standard deduction means that a person can lower their taxable income by a set amount per year and is a form of tax relief from the government—especially for those on the lower end of the income range. The standard deduction for the 2022 tax year is $12,950 for an individual and $25,900 for a married couple filing jointly. If Jordan has the same income as Skyler at $70,000 but doesn't have any of the deductions Skylar has, then he can still reduce his taxable income by $12,950, assuming he is filing as a single person, by taking the standard deduction. His new taxable income will be $57,050 ($70,000 - $12,950).

The government makes the rules on what is a valid deduction. Professional tax preparers will usually be on the watch for deductions on behalf of their clients, but it always helps to be aware of deductions that one might be eligible for. Further, a lot of tax filing software systems like TurboTax will ask about tax deductions, although it still takes research by the filer to know which ones to claim.

Tax credits work similarly to deductions but are in many ways superior. While a deduction lowers one's taxable income, and thereby reduces the amount they can be taxed on, a tax credit directly lowers the actual tax liability. To illustrate, let's consider the impact on Skylar of a $5,000 deduction relative to a $5,000 tax credit. Skylar makes $70,000. Without any deductions or credits, and assuming an average tax rate of 20%, Skylar would have a tax liability of $14,000 ($70,000 taxable income * 20% tax rate). With a $5,000 deduction, Skylar can lower her taxable income to $65,000. At the same 20% tax rate, her tax liability will now be $13,000 ($65,000 * 20%). She saves $1,000 on taxes by taking the deduction ($14,000 - $13,000). A tax credit, however, would apply the $5,000 savings directly to her original tax liability of $14,000, leaving her with a new tax liability of just $9,000 ($14,000 - $5,000). Skyler's got an extra $4,000 in her pocket relative to when she took the deduction.

Again, the government specifies which tax credits a person is eligible for, but because of the power of credits, savvy personal capital allocators should always be on the lookout for new ones they might qualify for.

A Large Cup of Tax Optimization

The reason I talk a lot about tax efficiency and not at all about tax evasion is simple: Tax evasion is illegal. I'll repeat: Not paying taxes that are due is illegal. However, being smart about which taxes you pay and when, with the goal of maximizing after-tax cash flow, is perfectly legal and might just make a whole lot of sense, depending on the situation.

For example, given the choice between selling a security in which we have a gain on day 364 of owning it versus waiting until day 366 in order to convert that profit to a long-term capital gain (and hence a lower tax rate), we might be inclined to wait the extra two days to significantly lower the taxes due upon sale. The difference is important. We are trying to be smart on taxes but not jump out of the way of them completely or try to convince them that you have skipped town and they should delete your phone number. After all, the IRS has caller ID, and I haven't skipped since my hopscotch days.

Over the next few pages, we uncork some thoughts and strategies to live more tax efficiently.

Invest Through Tax-Advantaged Accounts

Probably the number one way in which someone can lower their long-term tax liability is to make full use of the tax-advantaged investment options that exist. These are mostly referred to as "retirement accounts." We're talking IRAs (Individual Retirement Accounts), 401(k)s (offered by an employer) and something called a Roth (which can either be in the form of an IRA or a 401(k)). These specialized investment accounts are purpose-built for retirement saving and allow one to grow their wealth while deferring or eliminating entirely the taxes on profits that accumulate. The accounts differ a bit in their function, but the bottom line is that maximizing the amount of savings flowing into these accounts should grow wealth faster than in a regular brokerage account because of the tax advantages.

Let's see how this works, starting with regular or "traditional" IRAs or 401(k)s. By the way, 401(k)s are just a type of IRA that is administered by a company for the benefit of its employees. I refer to these IRAs and 401(k)s as traditional to differentiate them from Roth IRAs and 401(k)s, which we discuss next. In these two types of traditional retirement accounts, income is contributed before it is ever taxed, otherwise known as contributing "pretax" dollars. For those who use 401(k)s offered by an employer, a quick look at one's pay stub should show a line item for 401(k) contributions that are taken out of the paycheck and deposited into the 401(k) investment account. This happens before taxes are paid, so it is a deduction from taxable income that lowers what we owe in taxes during the period. If someone is using an IRA, they can contribute with whatever cash they have on hand and at the end of the year will be able to deduct this contribution from their taxable income. It has the same effect that the 401(k) contribution has by lowering tax liability and treating the investment contributions as pretax. To reiterate, the money we put into a traditional IRA or 401(k) has never had taxes paid on it.[45] What's more, taxes on investment profits earned in a traditional IRA or 401(k) are deferred until we take the money out. Here's an example.

Let's take things back to Maria, our Marketing Strategist. Maria is a serious saver, accumulating roughly $11,000 per year after paying her expenses. Let's say she contributed $1,000 of that into an IRA. By doing so, she can deduct $1,000 from her income and therefore lower her tax bill for that year by $1,000*35%, assuming her income is taxed at 35%. This

---

[45] And, if we put money into the account from our savings instead of having it automatically deducted from a paycheck, we can simply deduct this from our income at year-end and get a larger tax return.

is a $350 tax savings in the year that she contributes to her IRA. If Maria had been investing through a 401(k) plan sponsored by her employer, this $1,000 contribution would have been taken directly out of her paycheck and her taxes would have automatically gone down in unison.

Now, suppose Maria buys stock in a new consumer products company with a line of rainbow-infused soft drinks (zero sugar, 8 grams of fiber, guaranteed to get likes on social media). Sometime in the future, Maria sells this investment for $5,000. She made five times her money (taste the rainbow?). Normally, Maria would owe taxes on her gain of $4,000 ($5,000 sale price minus $1,000 cost). However, since this investment was made through an IRA, no taxes are due yet. Instead, when Maria withdraws this money, which could be many years away, she will pay taxes on the entire amount (the full $5,000). Remember, she never paid taxes on the original $1,000 she contributed because she deducted it from her taxable income, and she hasn't paid taxes on the $4,000 investment profit either. So, it makes sense that she will owe taxes on the full $5,000 eventually. If her tax rate at that time is 35%, then Maria will be left with $3,250 ($5,000*0.65).

The benefit is that she can defer these taxes until she withdraws the money from her account. This allows her wealth to compound a lot quicker than it would if she were just investing in a regular (non-tax-advantaged) brokerage account. Maria gets to invest more money today since she doesn't have to pay the government any taxes yet. Her wealth will benefit from the profits she earns on those extra dollars. Additionally, her tax bracket—and therefore the tax rate on those retirement dollars—may be lower in the future, depending on when she stops working and her income at that time. If her tax bracket today is 35% but her tax bracket in the future is 20%, then it makes sense to wait and pay taxes at the lower rate. The catch, of course, is that she doesn't know what her tax rate will be in the future. If only she had a crystal ball.

Readers may already be familiar with another type of retirement account called a Roth. A Roth is a specialized type of IRA or 401(k) account in which taxes are paid up-front rather than at the time of withdrawal. One way to think about this is that a Roth IRA or Roth 401(k) works in reverse. Instead of waiting until you withdraw to pay taxes, you pay taxes right at the beginning and then never again.

For example, let's say Maria earns a $1,000 bonus at year-end, and instead of contributing to a traditional IRA and deducting it from her taxes, she chooses to pay her income tax of 35%. This leaves her with $650 ($1,000*0.65). These are after-tax dollars. She now has the option of putting this $650 into a Roth IRA or Roth 401(k). Once it is in there, she will never have to pay taxes on it—or on the investment profits she earns— as long as she doesn't withdraw too early. Let's say she makes the same investment in the rainbow-infused soft drink company as above. Recall, that investment earned a 5x return, which means she will have turned her $650 into $3,250. This is a gain of $2,600 ($3,250 - $650). She can withdraw the full $3,250 without having to worry about sending a check to the IRS.

Notice that this $3,250 of after-tax wealth is the same result we derived above in the traditional IRA and 401(k) example. This is no accident. The reason we got to the same number was because the beginning and ending tax rates were the same at 35%. This points to a key takeaway about traditional IRAs and 401(k)s vs. Roth IRAs and 401(k)s: The tax rates are the driving force for which account will create the most wealth. If tax rates are high today, and we expect them to be lower in the future, we would want the traditional IRA, because we will pay taxes in the future at the lower rate. On the flip side, if tax rates today are low, and we expect them to rise in the future, we might choose the Roth option and pay taxes now, knowing that if tax rates in the future go up we won't have to worry. We can withdraw tax-free. Changes in tax rates over time can lead to either the Roth or the traditional retirement account offering a better deal or not.

By contrast, if she had invested through just a regular (non-tax-advantaged) brokerage account, she would owe $910 in taxes (assuming a 35% tax rate) on her gain of $2,600, leaving her with just $2,340 ($3,250 - $910). More than $3,000 with the traditional IRA and the Roth, and less than $2,500 without it. No brainer.

With the icing on top for retirement accounts, many employers will match contributions to a 401(k) account up to a certain limit, say 5% of one's salary. So, if a person earns an $80,000 salary, and is able to contribute $4,000 (or 5%) into a retirement account, their employer will send another $4,000 to the account. This is like getting a free 5% raise. Again, no brainer.

Figure 7.2 below shows the different retirement accounts in action compared to investing through a regular brokerage account. Notice how the after-tax wealth changes based on the ending tax rate.

Wealth Accumulation in Different Investment Accounts				
	Regular Brokerage Account (non-tax-advantaged)	Traditional IRA or 401(k)	Roth IRA or Roth 401(k)	Notes/Formulas
Income	$1,000	$1,000	$1,000	
Taxes today (35% tax rate)	-$350	$0	-$350	Income * tax rate
Contribution to account	$650	$1,000	$650	Income - taxes today
Investment gain	5x	5x	5x	
Ending account value	$3,250	$5,000	$3,250	Contribution * investment gain
Gain on investment	$2,600	$4,000	$2,600	Ending account value - contribution
Taxes on sale (35% tax rate)	-$910	-$1,750	$0	For Regular Brokerage: 35% tax rate on gain; For Traditional IRA/401(k): 35% tax rate on entire account; For Roth: no taxes due at withdrawal
After-tax wealth at 35% ending tax rate	$2,340	$3,250	$3,250	Ending account value - 35% taxes on sale
After-tax wealth at 20% ending tax rate	$2,730	$4,000	$3,250	Ending account value - 20% taxes on sale
After-tax wealth at 40% ending tax rate	$2,210	$3,000	$3,250	Ending account value - 40% taxes on sale

Figure 7.2: Wealth accumulation in different investment accounts.

There are some trade-offs to putting money into a retirement account. The biggest is the liquidity: Once the money is in, it is really hard—or financially painful—to get it back out. Some of this is mitigated with a Roth, because you can withdraw your contributions at any time. Remember, you've already paid taxes on those contributions. So, if you contribute $10,000 and it grows to $30,000, you can withdraw the original $10,000 without paying tax or a penalty. Withdrawing the remaining $20,000, however, would trigger taxes and an early withdrawal penalty, because you've never paid taxes on that money. Another potential option on the liquidity front is to take a loan out from your retirement account, although this is only available in certain situations. You'd have to pay the money back with interest, but at least it wouldn't trigger any additional expenses.

A Word From Michael: Roth And Traditional IRAs

From a tax perspective, when deciding on which IRA (Roth or traditional IRA) is better for you, consider your overall tax picture—not just the current year deduction that you receive for a traditional IRA contribution. This is influenced in large part by your expected future income and tax bracket. Remember, contributions to a traditional IRA aren't taxed on the way in, but you will pay taxes when you finally withdraw the money. For a Roth it is the opposite—you pay tax at the outset but do not owe any taxes at the time of withdrawal. So, if you expect your tax bracket in retirement to be lower than it is now, then a traditional IRA may be the right choice because when you eventually pay taxes, it will be at a lower rate than you are currently paying on your income.

The key, once again, is to think like an investor and maximize wealth rather than have the sole goal of minimizing taxes. Investing through a traditional IRA means you can put more money to work today because those dollars go in tax-free, but it also means you will owe a larger amount of taxes later on. Most of the time, the Roth investment will mean a lower overall tax bill because you pay taxes today on a smaller amount—your initial contribution—than will be available in the future once your retirement account has grown through investing. For example, it will require less tax dollars to pay income tax on $1,000 of income today than on $10,000 of future value after 20 years of investment returns. In exchange, by paying taxes today you won't be able to invest as much as you could with a traditional IRA. Puts and takes abound, but your tax rate today relative to your tax rate in the future is a key decision factor in choosing a Roth or traditional retirement account. Because of the uncertainty of future tax rates, many investors hedge their bets by putting money into both a traditional IRA and a Roth.

Income restrictions are also something to keep in mind when evaluating retirement accounts. Both traditional and Roth IRAs have some sort of income-based restriction. These could cap the amount you can contribute to a retirement account (a contribution limit) or disallow you from investing altogether (an income limit). Investors who earn above the income limit may be locked out of investing directly in a Roth, leading some to use a strategy called a "backdoor Roth." With the backdoor Roth, investors first put after-tax money into a traditional IRA, and then convert that money into a Roth account.[46]

This tax strategy, as with all tax strategies, depends on your income tax bracket, current income, and future income. The higher your current tax rate relative to your future tax rate, the less advantageous a Roth may be. In addition, there are some other nuances to doing the conversion that require a bit of thought. In complicated situations such as this, sitting down with a financial planner or CPA to develop a comprehensive framework for retirement saving can go a long way.

In addition to retirement accounts, there are some other tax-advantaged savings and investment accounts to be aware of. A Health Savings Account (HSA) allows one to put money aside tax-free for eligible healthcare expenses and can be a great way to fund out-of-pocket healthcare costs. A 529 Plan allows one to put aside money that can grow tax-free to pay for a child's higher education expenses. This is a real winner because of the multiplier effect on one's wealth that getting a high-quality

---

[46] One thing to note with this strategy is that you won't be able to deduct your traditional IRA contribution from your taxes if you exceed the income limit for that type of account.

education can have. If the kid ends up studying tax accounting, it is a triple whammy.

In Taxable Accounts, Be Mindful but Not Too Mindful

Taxable accounts are just another word for an investment account that has no special tax advantage. Opening a regular brokerage account is an example. There are several reasons why one might invest through a taxable account rather than through the tax-advantaged accounts discussed in the previous section. As we saw in "A Word From Michael," there are annual contribution limits for IRAs and 401(k)s, meaning that once a certain amount of money has been invested—$6,000 for an IRA in 2022, for example—no more can be added. There are also income limits, meaning that once a person reaches a certain income threshold they can no longer contribute to tax-advantaged accounts. A good problem to have. Third, there is the liquidity issue we mentioned—a person may not want to tie up their money until retirement.

Taxable accounts are, by definition, less tax efficient. But that doesn't mean that smart tax tactics (say that five times fast) can't be employed to improve results. We've already examined one method for lowering tax liability—converting short-term capital gains to long-term capital gains. As a reminder, capital gains are another word for investment profit. When those profits are earned over the course of a year or less, they are considered short-term by the IRS. Anything over a year is long-term. Short-term capital gains are taxed as if they were ordinary income that was earned through a job. That is, if Maria earned a $50,000 salary and also recognized a $10,000 short-term investment gain, then she'd pay taxes on the full $60,000 the same as if it all came from her job. Long-term capital gains, however, are taxed at a lower rate—currently 20% for the federal portion for people in the highest tax bracket.[47] This means that going from a short-term gain to a long-term gain could save a considerable amount. If the short-term rate is 35% and the long-term rate is 20%, then we could save 15% of the profit by waiting a year to sell. Of course, there are risks and other trade-offs to waiting.

Harvesting tax losses is another way that investors in taxable accounts pay less. This method involves selling something you have a loss on, and either buying something similar or waiting 30 days and re-entering. The goal is to be able to recognize a loss on this year's tax return without impacting the long-term performance of the portfolio.

Let's say Maria took a flyer on an aluminum can manufacturer headquartered in Denver (Plastic is out. Save our oceans. Plus, aluminum is fun to say). She's down 50% on her $1,000 investment (the CEO of this company may be canned by the board). If she knows of another, similar, aluminum can maker headquartered in Wichita, she can sell the Denver one for $500 and buy $500 of the Wichita one. As a result, this year she can deduct the $500 loss on her taxes ($1,000 Denver investment - $500 proceeds). If the tin can industry turns around, it is likely that the Wichita manufacturer will do similarly well as the Denver one (they should be highly correlated). Her $500 investment could go right back to $1,000, but she's harvested a tax loss and reduced her current-year tax liability in the meantime. What's more, she now has the option of holding onto the Wichita investment and deferring paying taxes on that investment until she sells. Finally, she can really juice her wealth by using the cash savings from her lower tax liability to add to her investment portfolio.

Taking long-term positions in companies with attractive areas of reinvestment is another interesting way to be extremely tax efficient. In

---

[47] Additional state and local taxes may apply.

Phase 3, we looked at dividends as one way that investors profit. Dividends, however, are sometimes taxable as ordinary income, meaning the same as if you earned that cash flow from a job.[48] Additionally, receiving the dividend is a taxable event that specific year, meaning there is no way to defer the taxes due. On the other hand, if companies have a lot of good investment options themselves, they aren't likely to pay much in the way of dividends. Berkshire Hathaway has never paid a dividend, for example. If a company doesn't pay a dividend, then unless one sells the stock, they never pay taxes because there is no taxable event. They haven't realized the gain because they never sold, and they have no dividend to report. They can benefit from the long-term growth of the company without having to worry about sending checks to Uncle Sam. Even if the investor eventually sells the position, they at least benefit from being able to defer the taxes between when they buy and sell, rather than paying taxes in the same year that dividends are received. Lowering tax payments today because of the deferral means that more can be invested, leading to greater wealth in the future.

One thing perhaps to keep in mind in taxable accounts is not to get too cute with minimizing tax liability. After all, taxes are only owed on profits, and earning profits is the primary reason for investing. Tax management can be helpful to returns, but it can also be a distraction or cause us to make decisions with poor economics, such as holding onto something we lose conviction in as an investment, just because we don't want to generate a taxable event. As with everything, there is a balance.

---

[48] Interested readers should research the difference between qualified and nonqualified dividends.

A Word From Michael: The Tax Refund

Heavy marketing from the likes of H&R Block and Turbo Tax has embedded in the American psyche that tax time is a windfall payday. Money that is just given to you by the federal government. REFUND!

One of the most difficult concepts to get across to clients is that you should not desire an income tax refund. Most taxpayers view tax time as their opportunity to come into a chunk of money, not realizing that it is their own money and that it is being returned to them by the government. I have actually had clients have withholdings taken out of their pay—knowing that their tax liability at year-end is zero at the moment—in order to get a refund that year.

Upon hearing this, I usually ask the client where they grocery shop. Many times, their response is Kroger. Fine, let's say that each week you shop at Kroger. The cashier rings up your items each time for a total of $200, then the cashier asks you to pay $250—an extra $50 that comes with no benefit. No worries, Kroger will refund you $2,600 at the end of the year ($50*52 weeks). What would you say to that? Of course not! Why overpay for something and receive no benefit? I then explain to them that that is exactly what you are allowing the taxing authority to do when you do not properly tax plan.

What you are actually doing at tax time is figuring out if you overpaid or underpaid on your taxes over the course of the year. However, many people don't see it this way.

Many clients of mine unfortunately struggle to amass savings, not realizing that there could be opportunities to save in the way they approach their tax returns.

An example will help illustrate.

Mr. & Mrs. X are clients. Mrs. X works as a cashier at Home Depot, Mr. X is unemployed, and they have one daughter who is seventeen. Mrs. X makes $33,000 per year. Looking at Mrs. X's W-2 I noticed that box 12D, normally used for 401(k) contributions, was blank. She wasn't able to save for retirement. The client's income is constant, always in the low $30,000 range. This particular year, the client's tax liability was only $373, yet they were receiving a $4,270 refund as a result of—among other things—taking the standard deduction ($24,800 for a married couple that year), a family tax credit of $500 for their daughter, an earned income tax credit of $2,256, and withholding tax of $2,360. This last part is important—the client had already paid $2,360 in taxes during the year which was taken directly from her paycheck. At the end of the year, she was receiving even more than this ($4,270) back in a refund.

I asked the client what they did with their tax refund every year. Their response was: "He likes his toys." Time to like financial independence! Both Mr. and Mrs. X wanted to save but just didn't see what was right before them. Surprisingly, they did not have any outstanding loans to pay down, nor did they have any consumer debt. After reviewing their tax return with them, I explained that $2,360 of their own money was part of their refund. The entire withholding amount from Mrs. X's W-2 that she paid throughout the year was being returned to her through her refund. In essence, she had loaned the government $2,360 for free that year. Very generous of her.

My advice was simple: Tell your employer that you are exempt from federal tax. Once her employer stopped withholding federal tax from her paycheck, Mrs. X could contribute 7% of her income to her employer-sponsored 401(k) plan. As a bonus, her employer matches up to 3.5% of pay, meaning that Mrs. X could be contributing a total of 10.5% of her salary—or $3,465—into a 401(k) each year. This is huge!

If these contributions were compounded over the remaining 22 years of her working life until she is eligible for social security benefits, Mrs. X would—using a 10% annual return estimate—amass a nest egg of almost $250,000. And this is just the withholding that she was giving to the government for free. It doesn't even account for whatever tax refund might remain, which could push this family's nest egg well past $300,000 if invested correctly. In this case, a couple that thought they couldn't save could be on their way to a significantly improved retirement—all with a little tax planning and reengineering their withholding strategy.

Maximize Deductions and Credits:

We've already taken an in-depth look at how deductions and credits work, so I won't repeat that here. However, in terms of tax optimization, making sure one gets the full amount of deductions and credits that one is eligible for can go a long way to lowering tax liabilities. Being lax in this area is leaving money on the table. Don't be lax about tax—make sure you get the max! (If someone from H&R Block is reading this, feel free to use that as your new slogan).

Use Real Estate to Your Advantage:

Real estate can be an efficient vehicle through which to build wealth while keeping tax liabilities to a minimum, whether through primary homeownership or becoming a real estate investor.

Homeowners might find that attractive incentive programs are available, such as for installing solar panels or heat pumps. First-time homebuyers may also be eligible for specific tax credits that make it easier to get your foot in the door (shoes off once inside please). Further, both mortgage interest and property taxes are usually deductible for tax purposes. This is one of the biggest deductions many households make during tax time.

In addition, real estate investors benefit from being able to deduct depreciation expenses on their taxes. Depreciation can mean different things, but in this context, depreciation means a specific deduction that real estate investors can take to lower their tax liability. These depreciation deductions are supposed to account for wear and tear on the property. For tax purposes, the property is seen as declining in value over time, so investors get to deduct these "losses" from their taxable income. In reality, however, properties typically increase in value if well-maintained, and so many times these depreciation "losses" are larger than the actual repair and upkeep costs which they are supposed to cover. Depreciation is also what's known as a non-cash expense, meaning that even though you are telling the IRS you have suffered a loss, there is no actual cash outflow associated with it. This is in contrast to other expenses, such as paying a property manager to oversee your investment. The tax savings from being able to deduct depreciation can be invested to supercharge wealth accumulation. Again, nuances abound.

A Word From Michael: Taxes And Real Estate Investing

Real estate investing can be a great, tax-efficient way to build wealth and generate income. Income from real estate investing is largely considered passive and is not subject to payroll or self-employment taxes—only income tax. Assuming you can mortgage the property and find a tenant, then the tenant is building equity for you by slowly paying off your mortgage with their monthly payments. After sufficient equity is built, this property could be leveraged into down payments for additional properties—either by refinancing to take cash out or by selling. The first property pays for the second, the second pays for the third, and so on. A real-life game of Monopoly®.

Further, because of depreciation deductions, rental real estate can generate positive cash flow—the actual amount of dollars coming in or out—while still allowing the investor to take a loss for tax purposes, thereby lowering overall tax liability. Remember, depreciation deductions are non-cash, but the tax savings from them are very real.

There are some quirks to the tax code when it comes to real estate (surprise, surprise). For example, it is not always the case that losses on rental properties can be used to reduce taxable income in the year they occur. Depending on the situation, these losses could be suspended—meaning deferred—until the property is sold. Whether or not this happens is dependent on—among other things—one's level of participation in the real estate investment (such as collecting rents, performing repairs, listing the property, etc.), as well as the presence of passive gains on other investments (such as stocks, bonds, or other real estate properties). These are called passive activity loss limits, for anyone who'd like to do further research.

Passive activity loss limits do have a couple of exceptions, namely for those qualifying as a real estate professional[49] or those actively participating in the real estate business.[50] Clearly, this can get complicated. Working with a professional advisor who is knowledgeable in this area could pay dividends.

---

[49] If you are a real estate professional, then your rental real estate activities are considered ordinary income and are not passive.
[50] The IRS defines active participation as collecting rents, coordinating repairs, or performing repairs, listing the property for rent, showing the property, etc. If a taxpayer owns at least 10% of a rental property and actively participates in management, then they can likely deduct up to $25,000 in rental losses. The losses can be taken against ordinary income but are phased out once income exceeds $100,000 and lost completely when income exceeds $150,000, at the time of writing.

Another potential source of tax savings for real estate relates to property tax assessments by local municipalities. Governments that collect property taxes need to have a way to value the homes in their jurisdiction, so they know how much property tax to charge each home. However, just because an assessment suggests a value for one's home doesn't mean that the homeowner has to accept it. If one feels that their assessment is too high and that their home is worth less than its valuation, there could be a chance to contest it and get the property tax bill reduced. In this weird scenario, homeowners are trying to prove that their house is worth less than what other people say it is. This concept could make for a good game show someday. Should we call it Home Floppers?

Miscellaneous

Renounce U.S. citizenship and move to Antarctica. I jest. Plus, the penguins have instituted some sophisticated and progressive fish taxes. However, moving to a low-tax jurisdiction is certainly one way to reduce taxes. States have varying levels of tax packages. Many states don't have an income tax at all. With telecommuting a much more viable option than it has been in the past, moving to a low-tax state might lead to savings on the bottom line assuming one's company doesn't reduce pay for living in a lower-cost area. This could be especially true for self-employed individuals who work online.

Another miscellaneous idea is to plan large taxable events for years in which one's tax bracket is particularly low. Let's say Jordan has a $20,000 unrealized investment gain on a stock but also expects to quit his job and travel for six months next year. This year, if he sells the stock, he will have to recognize the gain while he is still in a relatively high tax bracket. If he waits until next year, he might be able to save on taxes due to his lower tax bracket (he isn't working for half the year). Timing taxable events to fall during periods of low income can save quite a lot of unnecessary tax payments, assuming there aren't other reasons to trigger the taxes earlier.

Advocating for fiscal responsibility is an oft-overlooked way to reduce taxes for society, which will eventually flow back into one's pocketbook. Electing representatives who understand capital allocation and return-on-investment and are more discerning with the government checkbook could lead to more efficient government spending and a lower tax burden for citizens.

Last on the miscellaneous list is to bring in help. Taxes can be hard, and hiring a tax planner could save more money than it costs, in the long run. The larger and more complex one's tax burden, the more likely it would make sense to call a professional.

A Word From Michael: Tax Planning

When clients begin tax planning, their goal tends to be lowering their tax bill. However, proper tax planning isn't about lowering tax liability; it's about maximizing after-tax cash flow and wealth.

Here's a simple example. Let's say Bill and Samantha have the exact same financial profile– same income, expenses, and assets—except for one big difference: Bill has a mortgage on his house and Samantha doesn't. Bill will be able to deduct interest on his mortgage from his taxable income, thereby lowering the amount he will pay the government in taxes and increasing his year-end refund. Samantha, on the other hand, won't get the benefit of this deduction. Samantha owns her home free and clear, so she has no mortgage interest to deduct. Samantha's tax bill will be higher and her year-end refund will be lower. But would she trade places financially with Bill? Of course not! Samantha is wealthier, even though she pays more in taxes.

Sometimes, focusing too closely on lowering tax liability can negatively impact wealth accumulation. Let's say Brenda and Sue are in a similar financial situation and each has

$100,000 to invest. Brenda, mostly concerned with lowering her tax liability, chooses to invest her $100,000 in a tax-free municipal bond that pays 2% at the end of the year. With her 2% interest, Brenda would have $102,000 at the end of the year with a tax liability of zero. She's managed to earn some profits without paying taxes because the municipal bonds are tax-free.

Sue, however, decides to invest her $100,000 in an S&P 500® index fund, which is not tax-free. Using the average annual return of the index—estimated at 10%—Sue would expect to have about $110,000 by the end of the year. Let's say Sue sells a day before year-end and now has a short-term capital gain of $10,000 ($110,000 - $100,000). Using a short-term capital gains tax rate of 20%, Sue would pay federal tax in the amount of $2,000 ($10,000 * 20%). After paying taxes, Sue has $108,000 left over. Sue has a $2,000 tax liability to pay, while Brenda's tax liability is zero, but at the end of the year, Sue has $108,000 after tax and Mary has $102,000. Sue ends up wealthier because she focused on maximizing after-tax cash flow rather than minimizing tax liability.[51]

If being successful at the other parts of this book results in more money flowing to Uncle Sam, rejoice! A large tax bill, while unsavory, is typically a good problem to have because it means we are generating wealth. That said, hopefully this chapter has started to frame how tax efficiency can create lasting positive impacts on our pocketbooks—especially if we bought that pocketbook in New Hampshire. That is a win for everybody.

---

[51] Risk preferences and other considerations aside, for simplification purposes.

Toolkit Summary—Taxes

- Taxes exist to fund the government and can be thought of as an investment in Government, LLC.
- Taxes also function as an incentive system, pushing people to take certain actions they might not otherwise take.
- There are many different kinds of taxes. Municipal, state, and federal taxes are the key jurisdictional segments. Income, expense, and asset-based taxes are other important lenses through which to classify our payments to the government.
- The U.S .has a progressive system for its income taxes that segments a person's income into tax brackets and applies a gradually rising rate to each bracket.
- Tax optimization can involve making full use of tax-advantaged investment accounts, being mindful of the implications of buying and selling in taxable accounts, maximizing deductions and credits, using real estate as a tax-efficient investment vehicle (or re-domiciling in Antarctica).

Acknowledgements

I began writing what eventually became *Working Capital* during the early months of the Covid pandemic in 2020. At roughly half past 9 p.m., and for no particular reason that I can remember, I stood up, walked down the hall to my laptop and started typing up the introduction. My girlfriend (now fiancée - !!) and I had fled our three-square-foot apartment in Manhattan, and were crashing at my parents' house, as many people were during that time. That we were sheltering alongside Mom and Dad turned out to be the perfect metaphor for this acknowledgement section, because I owe much of the completion of *Working Capital* to their support and guidance.

My mom, Wendy Nardi, just happens to be an amazing writer and editor who has been assisting authors for years through her consultancy, Nardi Editorial (get in touch if you have a project—she's currently accepting new clients). She was the X factor behind many of revisions one through thirteen—her fingerprints are all over the manuscript. What's more, my dad, Kevin Huffman, contributed the title after hearing me talk about the book for approximately 6.8 seconds.

My aforementioned fiancée, Abby Rutt, lent a wonderfully helping hand by reading the manuscript several times and offering a treasure trove of useful edits. She also motivated me to keep pushing the project forward despite being bogged down in the later revisions.

Countless others provided their thoughts, time, and encouragement to get this across the finish line by carefully reading the different versions and helping me improve upon the material. I'm grateful to Mikhiel Tareen, Vic Cunningham, Jake Turkowski, Andrew Avitable, Stephen Dodd, Mia Nardi-Huffman, Abigail Hornstein, and Kon-Yao Kwek.

Rebecca Fretty of Firebird Branding gave me a great overview of how the self-publishing machine works.

Last but not least, those of you who made it through the Tax section have already met my cousin, Michael Elias, whose thoughts about saving and investing have been instrumental to me for years. As a CPA, he also collaborated heavily on the tax portion of the book.

INDEX

ABOUT THE AUTHOR

Gabriel Nardi-Huffman is a CFA charterholder and Senior Analyst at a private investment firm in New York, where he searches for, analyzes, and pitches investment ideas spanning a range of sectors and geographies. He loves digging into new companies and industries to uncover interesting investing situations. A lifelong investing enthusiast, Gabriel grew up in Norwalk, CT, and studied Math and Economics at Wesleyan University, where he also played lacrosse and occasionally danced at parties. He lives in Brooklyn, NY, with his fiancée Abby. To learn more about Gabriel, or to connect with him, check out www.myworkingcapital.xyz or e-mail him at hello@myworkingcapital.xyz.

Printed in Great Britain
by Amazon

38484650R00158